# ONLY THAT

# Only That

*The Life & Teaching of Sailor Bob Adamson*

KALYANI LAWRY

NON-DUALITY PRESS
An Imprint of New Harbinger Publications

ONLY THAT: THE LIFE AND TEACHING OF
SAILOR BOB ADAMSON

First paperback edition published July 2010 by
Non-Duality Press



Cover design by Kees Schreuders: case@ods.nl



Typeset in Berling

Non-Duality Press is an Imprint of

ISBN: 978-0-9563091-7-4
www.newharbinger.com

## Acknowledgements

My deepest gratitude to Bob in whose presence the story ended.

Special thanks to Barbara for her comments and insights.

To Bill Tys for casting his sharp eye over the manuscript.

To Tony Di Donato for the tidying up of the photos.

And to all who have offered their recollections and helped this book to fruition.

Thank you to my dear husband Peter without whom this book would not have been completed.

And to Julian and Catherine of Non-Duality Press for making this story available to all.

My love to each and every one.

# Contents

## Part 1 - The Life

## Part 2 - The Teaching

# Illustrations



Credits: *Page 57: (Alinta Farm)* Eric Magee. *Page 68: (Bob and Kalyani)* Tony Di Donato. *Page 70: (Bob at front door)* Kalyani Lawry.

## Foreword

"All phenomena are like the sky and the characteristic feature of the sky is its natural condition. Everything abides in this natural condition. No phenomena manifesting to perception can be altered from their authentic state.

"Nobody in the past who has set out on the path has reached the destination by persisting in seeking and striving. Nobody who has undertaken action has ever achieved the fruit. Nothing can be altered from the natural condition. All abides therein."

This quote, from a Dzogchen text from over two thousand years ago, points to the non-dual essence that has always and ever been just this and nothing else. That effortless recognition is the natural way of abiding. May the effortless recognition occur through the reading of this book, as it has in the writing expressing effortlessly through the pattern labelled Kalyani.

Bob Adamson
*Melbourne, Australia*
*March 2010*

PART 1

# The Life

## A Biography of Sailor Bob Adamson

## Preface

My first recollection of Bob Adamson arises from March 1974 as he walked into the large front room of a house in Melbourne, Australia, where Swami Muktananda Paramahansa was about to give an address to a gathering. The daily programme began in the early morning with chanting and meditation, then satsang in the late afternoon and chanting in the evening. For whatever reason, I noticed Bob. I often watched him come in and sit down. His attention was always very focussed and one-pointed as he found his place.

In the spirit of the times, a large number of those attending were young, long-haired and attired in Indian style clothes. Bob however was a proper looking man, upright, strong and roughly my parents' age – mid 40's. He had a woolly beard and sideburns and wore a little pink knitted beanie that looked distinctly at odds with his demeanour. The beanie had a very loose pom-pom that used to *bob* around, and that's how I remembered his name, though it is unclear how I came to know it in the first place. Each time he entered the room and sat down, I would look across to check if the pom-pom was still attached.

Muktananda visited the Adamsons' home in Ivanhoe for a satsang and my husband, Peter, and I were among those who filled the large front room to capacity. Bob and his wife Barbara continued to hold regular chanting evenings after the Australian tour finished. We next saw Bob at Muktananda's ashram in Ganeshpuri, India, in late 1975. Muktananda was away on an extended stay in America at the time and there were only a handful of westerners there. Jobs were allocated; I cleaned toilets and gardened while Peter worked in another section of the garden with a few of the men.

Peter recounts, "One morning I was assigned to work with Bob in the composting area of the garden, or shit pits as we called them. Bob and I were both turning the piles of rotting vegetable matter and mixing in elephant dung. We had just started for the day and, as Bob stuck his shovel in, a large king cobra slithered out. In India, the cobra is considered auspicious and believed to be a manifestation of Lord Shiva. But as an Australian, Bob instinctively jumped back, lifted his shovel and yelled, 'Shit! A snake!' With one quick strike he cut off its head, and then proceeded to dice it into pieces calling it a 'fucking snake.' People working nearby heard the commotion and came to investigate. The news circulated quickly around the ashram and they were quite dark on him for a while."

After Peter and I departed from Ganeshpuri, we bumped into Bob and fellow ashramite Mark West on a street in Bombay. They'd just come from the jewellers and proudly showed us their large pendants engraved with "*Sadguru Nath Marahaj ki jai.*" At that stage Bob talked about going to see Nisargadatta and invited us along. However, as we had plans to be at

Ramana Maharshi's ashram in Tiruvannamalai for Shivaratri, a religious festival, we declined.

There are all sorts of details about Bob that I recall from those days in the 1970's: the colour and features of the shirt he was wearing in Bombay, his habit of shifting weight from one foot to the other, his gaze which used to constantly move around and rarely settle during conversation, and his habit of turning his head to the side when listening. These days his energy is unwavering and constant, his bearing is steady, his gaze is direct and uninterrupted and he wears hearing devices.

Back in Melbourne in 1974 during Muktananda's visit, the Adamsons had lent their large rug to cover the bare floor of the satsang room. Bob had also contributed a large sum of money to help finance the tour. Perhaps some of that money paid for the advertising that drew Peter and me to the daily programmes and the opportunity to spend much of the day around Muktananda. It seems ironic that the carpet I remember sitting on as a 21 year old, and the carpet I sit on decades later, are both Bob's.

It's also now clear as to why I should remember him so well and in such remarkable detail, especially given that I have no recollection of any conversation with him. In the stillness, the oneness, the eternal, notions of past and present collapse into the emptiness from which they spring. Given this, where could forgetting be?

# Introduction

This short biography is woven out of the fragments of memories and reflections patiently offered by Bob and supplemented by his wife Barbara. The gathering, selecting and organising of these recollections attempts to illustrate Bob's *Bobness,* the unique human pattern vibrating and expressing as that particularised form. That *Bobness* is remarkably ordinary, yet profoundly extraordinary. There are some who recognise him, yet for the many, he remains unnoticed. Either way it doesn't matter.

What Bob refers to as *the understanding* is not something that is rare, nor is it the exclusive domain of the spiritual elite. It is the clear seeing that is available to all who care to really look. Bob invites those who come to listen to really *see* and get a taste of their true nature. He is keen to point out that it is not just for the few, it's for everyone. In the *seeing* that he speaks about, the illusory nature of what had been taken as the real simply loses its bind and there is nothing more to do. For those who do truly see, the search ends and there is a profound sense of what can only be described as *wellbeing* – a total freedom from all psychological bondage.

Meetings are held three times a week in the lounge room of the apartment in leafy Deepdene, Melbourne, that he shares with Barbara. They are informal gatherings, open for all to attend and run for about ninety minutes. Thrice weekly, an assortment of people arrives to listen, discuss and ask their questions. They sit on the couch, dining chairs, foldaway chairs or on the carpeted floor. There are often visitors from interstate or travellers from overseas who have made the long journey to spend time with him. The sessions usually begin with Bob giving an introduction on non-duality and then what follows is always unique and particular to that session.

Bob uses only a minimal number of concepts in his teaching and refuses any elaboration on them. Non-duality is spoken about as *One without a Second*. The word *second* is included to make it clear that there can be nothing more than the singularity. When someone attempts to add complexity, he immediately undercuts it and returns to the core. The very nature of the mind is to habitually embellish to produce even more. "Why complicate things?" he says. "After all, what can be simpler than one?"

When beliefs that had shored up the notion of being a separate entity begin to falter, glimpses of the oneness break through like sunlight between clouds. It is helpful when a fully awake person points to the fact that you are *That*. The talking that takes place in the room creates a slipstream that has the capacity to awaken that recognition. When asked by a newcomer one evening if he were a sage, Bob seemed bemused as he responded with words from the folk song, "No, I'm parsley, rosemary and thyme." The whole room cracked up laughing.

A line from the Genjokoan written by the founding Soto Zen master Eihei Dogen explains, "When Buddhas are truly Buddhas, they do not necessarily notice that they are Buddhas. They are actualised Buddhas, who go on actualising Buddhas." In the world of spiritual teachers, Bob is a rarity, a clear vessel. He has not allowed hierarchy and officialdom to evolve around him, nor a spiritual circus to develop. There is no darshan or blessing, for who could give what and to whom? When the meetings close, his farewell is simply a generous and heartfelt bear hug.

Bob exudes a very big and unwavering energy. His gaze is direct yet soft – a clear space is filled with love. He makes each feel as if they have a special relationship with him. Being tall and standing very upright, he is remarkably active for a man of his age. He can be exceptionally gentle and seems fearless, the kind of person you would want accompanying you if you had to walk down a dark alley at night. Over the years Bob has been accompanying many in their journey through darkness and some of those seemingly dangerous places. Perhaps he remembers those places from his own life.

His manner is usually polite. Bob has a correctness about him and he is uncompromisingly honest and acutely sensitive. He doesn't miss a thing. A sharp eye for detail and a natural sense of beauty are qualities that possibly formed from his close contact with nature as a child. His keen insights sometimes reveal themselves in a concise and dry wit. His niece Ottalyne recalls that he was always lots of fun because he amused the kids with his jokes.

Sometimes his wry summations serve to undercut any aggrandising which can creep into conversations about spirituality. He simply doesn't see anyone as spiritual, let alone more or less so than anyone else. Neither does he see anyone as *a someone*. He's quick to point out that everyone is *That* whether they know it or not, so what would all the fuss be about?

Bob is very focussed with any undertaking. It seems that this one-pointedness may have sometimes cut against the grain. Being an independently minded person, he has readily explored new ideas, many that were perhaps counter to much of the thinking of his contemporaries and which may have created some isolation from time to time.

Yet Bob is very matter of fact and can sometimes be quite blunt with a brusque, take it or leave it attitude. The qualities of being dogged and remaining one-pointed may have been the very qualities that served him in the process of discovering the truth. He simply wouldn't let the non-understanding rest. In the words of Zen Master Bassui Zenji, "What is obstructing realisation? Nothing but your own half-hearted desire for truth. Think of this and exert yourself to the utmost."

During the meetings, I've seen the occasional rudeness and impoliteness met on his part with compassion and generosity. The same question repeatedly asked by the same person over many months was always patiently met with Bob's genuine interest and fresh response. Yet if a situation arises which demands a forceful response, Bob can fire up and engage in some strong verbal debate.

He does not avoid conflict just for the sake of keeping the peace.

Bob is the last teacher for many and his meetings are truly a finishing school. When a visitor who had travelled from overseas said "My full stop is that you're the last teacher, this is it," Bob responded, "It better be. And cast this one out too."

Bob has fully realised his true nature. As he puts it, "There is nothing to do, nowhere to go and nothing to be." He is an equal with his beloved and final teacher Sri Nisargadatta Maharaj.

*Above:* Bob at two and a half years old on his pony

*Left:* Bob and younger brother Mervyn

## Early Life

Bob's family were not religious in any way and had no interest in anything spiritual. Born on the family farm on Saturday 21 July 1928, Bob's early years coincided with the Great Depression. These years were difficult for the family as they had gone through the hardship of severe floods and lost their farm. They had been in the process of selling the property when the government declared that all loans be frozen. The contract of sale had been signed and was legally binding, however settlement had not taken place and subsequently the money owing was never paid to his family.

Bob's father then became the manager of several farms in the Beaconsfield area owned by one of Melbourne's wealthy establishment families. While Bob's family didn't have a great deal, life was uncomplicated and free for the Adamson children. Bob, his two older sisters and younger brother spent much of their time exploring the surrounding bushland. They relied on each other's company and spent much of their time making their own fun and getting up to all sorts of antics. When they misbehaved they were "given a belting", yet Bob recalls his childhood as being good.

Bob's grandparents had settled in Beaconsfield quite early and some of their children remained in the region and had in turn married and had children. A veritable tribe of Adamson children attended the tiny local school. When he started school, it was a three mile walk for Bob, but as he got a little older, he rode a pony to school and later a horse. Bob pitched in around the farm helping with general duties including sheep dipping and crop harvesting. Once, when he was leading one of the draught horses back from pulling the farm machinery, it stood on his bare foot crushing it badly against the cobblestones. He became very good at riding and won a couple of medals in competitions. His eldest sister Noel said he was a skilful rider and that he could "ride the tail off a pony".

Bob didn't take easily to classroom learning, which was all the more difficult as he was naturally left-handed but was made to write with his right hand – a usual practice then. He was self-conscious about his handwriting and school learning became increasingly hard for him. Given Bob's sensitive nature, his astute eye for detail and his natural intelligence, there must have been an underlying frustration at not being able to put his interior landscape into words.

When school got out at 3.30 pm, the real learning began. Bob would catch rabbits, net eels, hunt lizards, kill snakes and collect other treasures. His Uncle Arthur was a close friend of the naturalist Charles Barrett. Arthur and Charles frequently went out observing the then abundant bird life of the region and recording data on numerous species including the now endangered Helmeted Honeyeater.

Accompanying his Uncle Arthur, young Bob spent a lot of time in the bush learning about the different birds and their calls. Over time, he gathered a large collection of their eggs. With the senses and intuition allowed free rein, his explorations led to an appreciation of the natural world around him; direct, real, factual and immediate.

At the meetings, when someone says that they understand *intellectually* what he is saying, he is quick to point out that you either understand something or you don't. "Two and two equals four: is that an intellectual understanding or do you know it for a fact?" Bob often draws on examples from the natural world to illustrate some of the points he is talking about. Such stories are filled with a warmth and beauty.

In 1940 when Bob was twelve, he and his family left the Beaconsfield farm and moved to Melbourne. His first job was delivering telegrams within the City of Melbourne. Two years later he left home and headed for the fruit picking camps. They were comprised of itinerant workers, "alcoholics, deadbeats, people on the run and no-hopers living in the huts and camps. There was boozing going on all the time. If you opened your mouth, you'd get a fistful."

That way of life presented a pretty rough transition to independence for a young adolescent. In order to survive he had to quickly learn to defend and protect himself.

Back in Melbourne in 1943 and at 15 years of age, Bob was taken to a pub one Friday night by two slightly older boys who worked with him. Bob said that he had three drinks and the world changed for him. Later, when he tried to recapture that euphoric state, he was unable to, because he would always drink past it.

This world of drinking that opened for him at this formative stage of his life would in the following seventeen years become one of darkness and despair and would almost destroy him. The precious years of his young adulthood became a blur and the social skills necessary for life had little opportunity to develop and flourish.

## Becoming a Sailor

With the Second World War underway, Bob, like other young men, was eager to sign up for military service. His father Robert, having fought at Gallipoli in the First World War, would not give permission for his son to join up. As one of the last stand of men who held on firing while the remaining group escaped to the Gallipoli mainland, he knew only too well what war entailed. So Bob had to wait until his seventeenth birthday to apply. Four months later, in November 1945, Bob was accepted into the Navy. The war had just ended but Bob was contracted for a full twelve-year term and was immediately sent off to Japan.

Bob began to look the part of a sailor and was tattooed by Rocky Vain, the Flinders Street tattooist. He has two on each arm, one on each leg and across his chest a serpent and eagle embrace in a combative struggle. His parents, grandmothers and a bevy of aunts and uncles were outraged.

The discipline of Navy life got to Bob, especially the abuse, unfairness and injustices meted out on a regular basis. Being "stood over" affected his sense of self-worth and there was a continuous cycle of drunkenness and getting into fights. A pattern of resentment built and he felt that life was against him and bitterly unfair. This belief rubbed raw against the events of daily life. While the alcohol anaesthetised this temporarily, it compounded the growing problem. There were many alcoholics in the Navy and boozing, abuse and fighting were simply a way of life.

Bob lasted about two and a half years of his term before being discharged. The charge for his expulsion was that he was a chronic alcoholic with anxiety neurosis. He was only nineteen years old and it had been a damaging experience. His hearing was also permanently impaired as a result of gun practice.

*Right:* The young Sailor Bob, Crib Point, Victoria, 1946

*Below:* Hong Kong, 1948

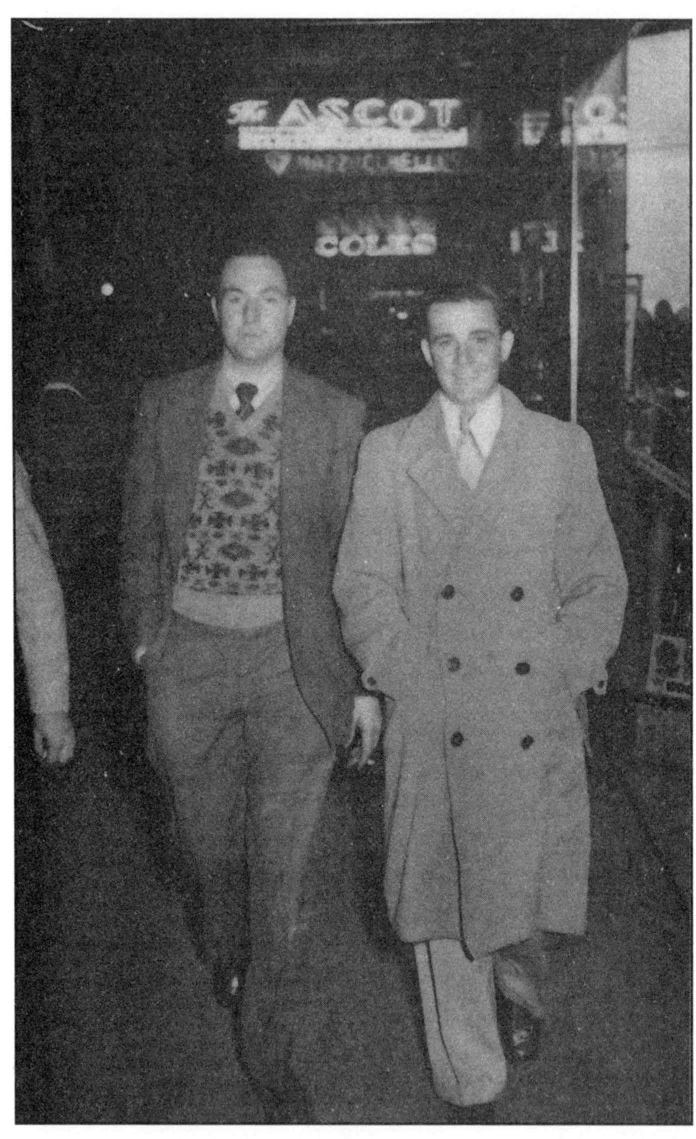


Bob (left) with a fellow shearer out on the town in South Australia *circa* 1952

## Going Shearing

After leaving the Navy, Bob worked on a farm in the Western District of Victoria. He was about twenty-one at the time and, being attracted to the idea of the backcountry of Australia, he travelled to Charleville in outback Queensland to try out at shearing. It took a while to learn to handle the sheep and in the initial stages his arms and back ached at the end of the day. He worked in numerous places in Queensland and would follow the shearing season down through New South Wales, Victoria and across to Tasmania.

"Queensland in January and February would be as hot as buggery especially working on the board under a low tin roof. You'd be sweating and struggling with the big wethers." At the end of shearing season Bob would often decide not to return to work in such conditions again, but when his money ran out he would contact the publican up there and be sent the fare. The publican knew that the money he lent the shearers would be recouped when they returned to the bar with their pay cheques.

Life as a shearer involved taking as much booze as possible out to the sheep station where it would be consumed within the first couple of days. A lot of shearers were alcoholics and when they arrived at the property they'd lie around in the huts boozing for the first few days before starting the shearing. Bob recalls,

"The contractor would be screaming his head off but we couldn't do anything about it – we were in the horrors. We used to call it 'zoo night' when the booze cut out. You'd start hallucinating all sorts of animals and there'd be a lot of screaming and yelling."

On Friday nights, exhausted from days of hard work, the shearers would pile into a vehicle and head straight to town. In the pub there would be exaggerated stories about the shearing accomplished in the sheds. Bob recalls that the shearers would "shear more sheep in the pubs than they did in the shed", while their wages would be spent in no time. There was a lot of hard drinking.

The shearer epitomises an aspect of the Australian national character and today is still iconic in the cultural imagination. These tough-minded blokes were fast on their feet with a self-deprecating humour, a dry wit with a turn of phrase often "too blue for the womenfolk". With regard to the shearers romantic lives, the saying was that they were always "Too tired, too drunk, too far away".

Apart from the obvious disadvantages, there was a sense of freedom in being a shearer. "In the shearing sheds you are your own boss. You were in a team with a contractor and back then the industry in Australia was small." Bob had a hard-earned reputation as being a "gun shearer" – a title earned by a very small number of shearers who are highly skilled, very fast and able to cut very cleanly. With bravado and rivalry rampant, a gun shearer was a highly respected figure in the fiercely competitive environment of the shearing shed.

Regardless of his drinking, he would always be wanted as the best and fastest.

He didn't get home to Melbourne very much as he was always off shearing somewhere. Yet through the ups and downs and no matter where he was in Australia, he always sent money home to his mother, Mary, who was a widow. His father was in his sixties when he died from complications that developed as a result of injuries sustained in a ploughing accident. Bob was very close to his mother and they loved each other a great deal. However, Bob's drinking problem, compounded by his increasingly difficult behaviour, led to an estrangement with other members of his family.

## Getting Sober

In an effort to quit drinking and make a new start, Bob took a ship over to Western Australia and applied for shearing work with one of the grazing companies up in North West Cape country. "Nobody knew me over there, so I intended to make a new start without the drink. A group of us was hired by the grazing company and picked up by a truck fitted with a couple of forms along each side for seats. We all threw our gear in and set off. Every town we'd come to we'd pull up and everybody'd get into the pub and start boozing."

"The driver would try to round everyone up. He'd start by rounding up two or three men and putting them on the truck and then he'd go around looking for some more. When he got back, the first two or three would be gone so in the end he said, 'Right, I'm not stopping at any more towns.' This didn't go down too well so as we were going past this town they said to him, 'Hey, hey, hello! There's a bedroll off – a bedroll's dropped off.' He replied, 'I don't care!' They called out and said, 'It's alright, it's your bedroll!' So of course he had to stop. So a trip that should've taken us a couple of days instead took us a week. Well that ended my period off the booze. As soon as I got on the truck with all the rest of them I was right into it again."

The plan to begin a new life without alcohol had failed. Bob then left Western Australia and travelled back to South Australia where he picked up work shearing. He and his mates would get gallon jars filled with "plonk" and they would drink themselves into oblivion. One of his friends suicided and that took Bob to a particularly low point. He recounts that he was full of self-pity and felt that the whole world was against him. He felt broken and any sense of self-worth had completely disappeared. He too considered ending his life. "I got into the horrors there and it got that bad I was going to shoot myself." It was a desolate emotional landscape and one filled with enormous despair.

Drinking unleashed a deep aggression and he could sometimes get violent. Brian Garrett, one of Bob's old shearing mates, said, "After Bob's tenth drink at the bar, he'd swing around and for no apparent reason would land a punch on the bloke sitting next to him." Bob said that, because he could sometimes become obnoxious when he was drunk, he had no steady relationships with any women and it would have been impossible then for any relationship to last.

The frustration of not having formed an articulate pathway through which to express himself made communicating difficult. Drinking was an attempt to dull the pain of the profound sense of isolation and in turn it exacerbated the problem. Bob says that our problems are always one of relationship; the relationship of a seemingly divided self, pitting itself against the notion of other. There is either a pushing away of things believed to be unpleasant and undesirable, or a desperate attempt to cling onto the things believed to be good and bring happiness.

The basis of this psychological suffering is thought-driven and is sustained by continually adding further painful thoughts. It's in seeing that there is absolutely no separation in the first place that the sense of an apparent split is resolved and the push and pull of the dance subsides. When it is seen that there is nothing to hang on to and nothing to be pushed away, there is no tension held and suffering indeed finishes.

Bob joined Alcoholics Anonymous (AA) to get sober. As an anonymous fellowship, only first names were used. There were a number of different Bobs there at the time: Geordie Bob, Manangatang Bob, Brighton Bob and Big Bob. As an ex-seaman, he was given the name Sailor Bob. Although he had stopped drinking, he was still trying to dry out and remained "crook from the grog". His hands trembled a lot and the only jobs he could get were in factories and foundries. He remembers that, on one occasion, the shakes were so bad that while he was pouring molten metal, it dripped into his boots and burnt deeply into his skin.

His attempt to break from alcohol lasted only a short while and then he resumed the drinking. He was able to pick up work in a saw mill, he went shearing, worked as a wool scourer, and stoked the steam engine in Bourke, N.S.W. Bob laboured down the Cobar mines and did whatever else was going. One summer in the Wimmera, Christmas Day was spent sewing up bags of wheat in the hot sun. Bob felt pretty resentful about his lot, especially given that his employer was "seated indoors at a big table, eating Christmas dinner and enjoying the celebrations".

When he was back again in Melbourne and needing a job, Bob decided to go to sea again. He had his papers from the Navy and applied at the shipping office where he was given a job on one of the coastal boats working mainly on deck. "It was great because the Maritime Union was one of the strongest unions in Australia at that time and we had good wages and conditions. If you got sacked out of a job, you'd be on the bottom of a roster. If there was nobody else in, they'd have to take you back on again. They were so strong that they could do that."

He had returned to sea on the sugar run, transporting sugar grown in Queensland to the Yarraville refinery in Melbourne. One night while unloading at the sugar wharf he got drunk. The ship was supposed to sail at 10 pm but Bob did not turn up until midnight. The crew were trying to get him on board but he was fighting and yelling and refusing to budge. It had been raining and when they eventually got him on deck he was covered in mud and sugar and staggered to his bunk. As the crew members would not sail without him, the ship had to stay tied up in port for an extra day at an enormous cost.

Early next morning Bob was summoned to the bridge to face the music. He was still very hung over and began arguing back at the captain. The yelling carried on for a bit and then, in a fit of anger, Bob grabbed hold of the table, ripped it up from its bolts in the floor and chased the captain around the room with it. It was an extraordinary occurrence and the consequence of this fiery outburst was no less than a lifetime ban from going to sea plus a very large fine that took time to repay.

"Even the union got sick of me, so they tore up my union book and I was barred from going to sea. In between that, I was getting locked up for drunkenness and all the rest of it; brawling, fighting and God knows what."

## A Second Chance

In the 1960's the Painters and Dockers Union had a notorious reputation and was linked to the criminal underworld. They were very powerful and virtually controlled the waterfront. One day Bob went to the Royal Mail Hotel where many of the members drank. He recounted his story of threatening the captain with a table to one of the painters and dockers that he knew. It was suggested he go and see the union's secretary Jimmy, and get a job with them.

Bob was then offered work but realised that he would have again been caught up in the same old pattern of heavy drinking and fighting. It was in that very moment that he made the decision. He simply left his drink on the table, walked out of the hotel and made his way home to his mother's house in Mordialloc. His very last drink was never consumed.

Bob was nearly thirty-two years old and began attending AA meetings again. Physically he was a mess, he weighed about 15 stones and walking even a short distance would have him in a sweat. "An old bloke at AA called Little Les used to pick me up in his car and cart me around the place for the first four or five years. Later when he got old, I carted him around for the last 5 years of his life." A number of people helped Bob at this time and he has always tried to repay the kindness shown to him where he could.

At much the same time there were two men he knew who had left AA and had tragically killed themselves. One jumped out of a window of what was the Federal Hotel in Collins Street, Melbourne, and the other shot himself. It was around this time that Bob got hold of a book *Sobriety and Beyond,* written by a Catholic priest. In the introduction it said, "We alcoholics are given a second chance at life."

This stopping was now a second chance. It hit him that if he was given this second chance, how well was he going to use it? The task of discovering what indeed had given him this second chance became the focus of his life and the momentum for the exploration. There was only one way he could use this second chance and that was to find out what it was that had given it to him.

In looking for the source of this second chance, Bob investigated many paths including Pentecostalism, Methodism and Christian Science. He was baptised with full immersion and also began attending mass. An important book to him at this time was *In Tune with the Infinite* by Ralph Waldo Trine. It helped him develop a more positive outlook on life. He would check the newspapers regularly for any notices about spiritual lectures and pick up any books he was drawn to. Some books he would often re-read, while those with no further pull would be put aside.

Bob is widely read and has a very good memory, often quoting passages of scripture and other ancient texts effortlessly. He has an intuitive grasp of their innate meaning and an ability to offer deep and incisive insights into the texts, as well as a warm, heart-felt understanding of them. In cleaning up his life, he also began to read about nutrition. A long held interest in healthy eating and physical exercise began at this time.

Bob (third from left) at the Maharishi's press conference, Melbourne Airport, 1964

Bob (left) in beanie with stepdaughter Felice (right) listening to Muktananda, Melbourne, 1974

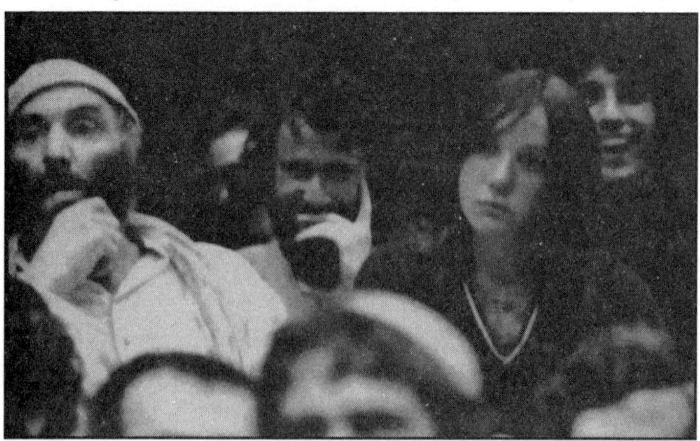

## Learning to Meditate

When Maharishi Mahesh Yogi came to Melbourne in 1962, Bob went and listened to him speak. The Maharishi was an exponent of mantra meditation, the practice of repeating a given mantra until the mind is stilled. When the mind becomes active again during the meditation, the mantra is again repeated until the mind has quietened.

Bob took up this idea and decided to do it off his own bat choosing the words *peace and love*. He repeated his mantra as suggested and continually reduced it until it merged. His mind quietened to a certain extent and he thought, "This is right – I've got it now." A few days later he saw a notice in the newspaper inviting people interested in yoga and spiritual matters to a meeting. He attended and listened to a tape of Maharishi's story and decided to be formally initiated with a given mantra.

"I went along to a room with a little table in the corner. I had to take along a piece of linen, some fruit and a week's wage which were placed on a table near a photo. I glanced at the photo only very briefly as I was nervously waiting to see what I was going to get. I sat quietly and a mantra was whispered in my ear which I started to repeat. After half an hour I got up and continued repeating it. I wasn't sure whether I was saying it correctly or not.

"A couple of days later as I was walking to the train station on my way to work, 'bang', it all lit up and there in front of me was a image of a man radiating light. The man was the one I noticed in the photo on the little table. He was Maharishi's guru." Bob recounts that at that time he didn't understand much about those sorts of experiences and thought he was being taken over by something. Yet he felt euphoric as if he could have walked off the highest building.

When he arrived at work that day several people asked, "What's the matter? Are you in love or something?" He replied, "Yeah," but it was the world he was in love with – it had suddenly looked different. Between 1962 and 1970 Bob continued with mantra meditation and also looked at some of Joel Goldsmith's teachings.

## Back at Sea

At an AA meeting some six years later someone suggested to Bob that he go back to sea. He replied that he wasn't able to because he'd been barred. It was put to him that he could go away as a steward. The money was very good at that time so Bob decided to follow up on the idea of returning to sea.

"Vic was the Secretary of the Maritime Union and he and I were old mates who had got the sack out of a ship together some years before for locking ourselves in a cabin and getting drunk. Anyway I went to see Vic and as I entered the room Vic looked up and said, 'No, not you. Anybody but you!' Another chap called Little Jock was also in the room and he said, 'Fair go, Vic. He hasn't had a drink for six years.' And so I started around Christmas time when there were vacancies due to many of the seamen taking holiday time with their families. The work involved doing the phosphate run from Nauru to Melbourne. It's a really deep port in Nauru and we had to wait for the tides to be right to get alongside. The ship would travel up there and then it would be seven or eight days sometimes before the ship could swing around to return." The ship was his home. The meals and accommodation were provided and Bob would spend much of his free time reading in his cabin. There was time for contemplation and the pay was good.

Bob and Barbara on their first date in 1968

## Meeting Barbara

Bob met Barbara in 1968 at the gym where she was working. At the time he was working as a steward on the Princess of Tasmania and when his ship was tied up in Melbourne he would exercise there. When Bob had the week off, they would go out together and their relationship began to develop over a period of time. Barbara recounts that Bob was impeccably dressed when he arrived to take her out for the first time, while she was struck by the fact that his clothing was so neat and smelt so clean. He was also very generous to her. Bob said that up until he met Barbara, there had been no special person in his life as he had no car to go out in or any assets to offer. His whole life then had been focused around sobriety and the spiritual understanding that was central to his living, "because without that I had nothing."

When they met, Barbara had just come out of a difficult marriage that had placed enormous financial and psychological pressure on her and she was working to support her four children. Bob says that he, as a recovering alcoholic, was also "still messed up". Bob had no experience of family life because much of his life had been spent in the bush or away at sea. He had no idea about bringing up children and this sometimes created conflict in the ready-made family. Given these circumstances, it is understandable that their relationship was difficult going at times and sometimes very fiery.

They married in 1973 and in the following years there were some separations. The emotional hurt from their split-up in 1975 may well have been the very fuel that propelled Bob to meet Nisargadatta, his final teacher. It had been an emotionally difficult time for him. The marriage had failed and he had severed himself from old friends. He left Australia in August of that year and went to live in India at Swami Muktananda's ashram in Ganeshpuri. Bob was absolutely one-pointed in his seeking. In a letter that he wrote to his mother, he said that he was not coming back to Australia until he had found the truth. The drive to resolve this painful sense of separation was a compelling force in his quest in understanding the actuality of "That, Thou Art".

Barbara recounts that, despite separations, the strong bond between them was never severed. In their relationship, when times were difficult and adversity was happening in the life they shared together, they supported each another and "functioned as one with such strength". A strong bond and deep love between Bob and Barbara is very apparent. Each is very much their own person; two very independent people sharing a life together. They care for each other in a myriad of little ways, with small tendernesses exchanged, a rebuke here or there, presumably the occasional shouting match, yet always a deep respect and profound loyalty between them.

Bob has been very supportive in the upbringing of Barbara's daughter and three sons and they in turn love and respect him. When granddaughter Romey was a baby, Bob cared for her while her mother Felice was at work. Romey and Bob share a very special bond and when a tiny girl, she gave him the name Bockie.

Bob cared for Barbara's father, John, during the last two years of his life. As his illness progressed and he became more dependent on Bob, there were sometimes fiery exchanges between the two men. They had a very deep mutual respect and Barbara said that not long before his death her father said to her, "I love that man."

## Siddha Yoga

Earlier, in 1970, Bob had been drawn to a photo of Muktananda in a newspaper advertisement and went to a meeting in Auburn Road at the home of Pat Stewart. Muktananda was from the Siddha Yoga lineage where *Kundalini* is awakened in the aspirant. Bob attended the meetings regularly and when Baba Muktananda came to Melbourne in that same year, Bob was with the group that greeted him on his arrival.

Four years later, he was part of the core group involved in organising Muktananda's next visit to Melbourne and in setting up the large house in Wellington Street, Kew, that had been rented for the tour. He arrived for the daily programme late in the afternoon after work and would sit in a focussed manner wearing the little beanie that Baba had given him. After Muktananda left Australia, Bob and Barbara hosted regular chanting and meditation evenings in their Ivanhoe home. Muktananda gave Bob permission to initiate others with *shaktipat*.

The teachings were central to Bob's life and he was very earnest in his meditation. Early in the morning he used to play a recording of Muktananda singing the Guru Gita. Bob said that listening to the voice stirred something deeply within him. He practised focusing his breath with the mantra, reciting sacred texts and chanting.

There were all sorts of spiritual experiences that arose including different sorts of visions as well as strong *kriyas* or spontaneous movements characteristic of activated *Kundalini*. He said that the teachings were the foremost thing in his life "because it gave me the life".

The practice was ongoing and after a while he got tired of the effort it required to maintain a particular state. "I still hadn't found out what it was that had given me the second chance, so that intensity was still there."

Photo of Nisargadatta taken by Bob, 1978

Bob and Barbara at Melbourne Airport before their return visit to India in 1978

## Nisargadatta Maharaj

Bob went to live at Muktananda's ashram on the outskirts of Ganeshpuri in India in 1976 after separating for a time from Barbara. He was one-pointed and devout in the daily programme which began early with meditation at 4.30 am, followed by chanting and *seva* or daily work. The beds were hard, the water for bathing was cold and the food was unimpressive.

Muktananda's guru was Bhagawan Nityananda and Bob used to sometimes undertake the customary washing of his statue with coconut milk. Nityananda had died in 1961 and his ashram, also in Ganeshpuri, was a place of pilgrimage. Bob had experiences of him in the subtle realm and would sometimes walk to the little ashram in the village and sit in his chair.

Seven months after moving to the ashram, Bob was visiting the Chetana Bookshop in Bombay and a shop assistant handed him Nisargadatta's *I Am That.* Friends at the ashram had offered him the book, but he was now drawn to read it. Nisargadatta's address was in the book, so Bob made his way to Vanamali Building, 10th Lane, Khetwadi, on 23 March 1976. He stayed on for a couple of days in Bombay to listen to further talks and over the next twelve months visited Nisargadatta as often as he could.

With little money, Bob's only way of staying in India was by living at the ashram. There was no charge, but daily work was expected. Short visits to Bombay were allowed, but extended stays away were not possible. When the opportunity to travel in to Bombay arose, Bob and Mark West would travel the two or three hour journey to attend Nisargadatta's talks.

Bob says, "Nisargadatta was from the Advaitan tradition and they break up awareness into consciousness, five sheaths, three *gunas* and God knows what. I suppose it's what you'd call a good way of explaining it. I don't belong to that tradition at all, or any other tradition. If you call it consciousness and try to create distinctions and point out different ways of its functioning – that's all very well. But in essence it's still one without a second, it's non-dual no matter how it appears.

"I keep it at that because I'd be well and truly lost if I started talking about the three *gunas* of consciousness and awareness and all the rest of it. Simply start from the fact that you're already *That* and stay with it. No matter what appears or not appears on it, it's the one. Whether it's consciousness, awareness, super-consciousness or sub-consciousness, all labels are purely conceptual.

"When Nisargadatta talks about 'I am beyond consciousness', people sometimes get the idea that there are different levels and there is more to it. What is beyond consciousness? What could there be and where would it be? Simply nothing – no-thing."

Bob was one of the first westerners to visit Nisargadatta's daily sessions after the translator of *I Am That,* Maurice Frydman, died. Nisargadatta used to say that Bob's invitations to other westerners were the cause of the influx. He would sit Bob at the front and sometimes their dialogues would turn into yelling matches. His pet name for Bob was Bhishma, the name of the great warrior in the Indian epic, Mahabharata. Bhishma lived to a very great age and Nisargadatta used to joke that although he was firing so many arrows at Bob, like Bhishma, he just wouldn't die.

Mark said that Nisargadatta loved Bob in a special way and would often provoke him. Sometimes Nisargadatta would look at Bob and teasingly ask, "What are you doing now, Bhishma? Trying to stay in the awareness?"

Bob recalls, "Nisargadatta would never agree to anything anyone ever said to him. As far as he was concerned, it was conceptual. Everything was a concept. I couldn't understand some of the things he was saying and I'd get frustrated and would argue and things would fire up. And there'd be a lot of shouting sometimes between us. I might have some answers to the questions but he'd knock them out and then I'd argue about that.

"He was taking away all my concepts and the dearly held beliefs and ideas of things that I thought I'd understood. He'd kick everything out from underneath me. And even though there might have been the seeing of the most profound truth, that simply wasn't good enough either. And the most sublime expression would be kicked out too. I was continually left with nothing. There was nowhere left to stand."

Nisargadatta told Bob that the only way he could

help anyone was to take them beyond the need for further help. And he did this by pointing out to Bob that he wasn't what he believed himself to be. "I wasn't the body or the mind and I could see that. What Nisargadatta was saying and continually pointing out was that it was all conceptual. The images, ideas and imaginings that I had about myself weren't the truth. I understood what Nisargadatta was pointing to."

Bob realised the essence of what Nisargadatta was saying the first time he saw him. He understood the mind was the problem and in clearly seeing it he thought he'd never get hooked in it again. Then at the end of the session, when he walked out the door and into the street, he immediately got caught up in the mind. It was different, though, because having seen that the problem was the mind, when he'd seemingly get hooked in, he'd say to himself, "Hey, wait a minute. This was seen through the other day; what's this about?" It would pull him up and he'd have another look and see that it was "just more of the same old mind crap".

"Those old habit patterns had been there for years and did not immediately stop," he said. "When the chatter of self-pity and resentment started up again, there was a remembering that actually there was nothing there and so it wouldn't last." Each time Bob saw the falsity, it would lose its intensity and the suffering began to ease off.

Bob sometimes uses a story to illustrate the point that when habits start to dissolve, the seemingly subtle becomes increasingly pronounced. He recounts that years earlier when he had started to give up smoking, the first handful of sunflower seeds he ate seemed bland with little taste to them. After a while without cigarettes, his tastebuds began to be able to discern the subtleties of the seeds. Likewise, the beliefs that had formed the notion of a separate "me" by imagining it was apart from the totality had seemingly clouded the very taste of the oneness. In the seeing through of this false notion of a separate "doer" who imagines it has volition and control, the numinous, the oneness, begins to be seen. "Start to get the taste of it," he says, knowing that once it is savoured there can be no forgetting.

Before going to Nisargadatta's, Bob used to meditate and do all the ashram discipline very earnestly, but that dropped away instantly. "Once you see that something is false, you can never truly believe it again. And if you can't believe it, how can you keep going back into it? Even if I'd never gone back to Nisargadatta it would have kept eating away and doing what it did anyway. Insights continued to come up and it got clearer in the discussions and arguments that Nisargadatta and I used to have.

"So there was nothing to do any more. Simply nothing to be, nowhere to go and nothing to see. I was in a sort of a limbo really. I had no motivation and might well have stayed in the ashram for the rest of my life. I wasn't moved to do anything or go anywhere and didn't know what direction to take. Then in early 1977 Barbara and her friend Muriel came over to India and during her five-week stay we met up and she attended

Nisargadatta's talks with me. We got back together and she returned ahead to Australia and organised my return ticket."

Nisargadatta was sad when Bob told him that he was leaving India. Just before Bob left, Nisargadatta arranged a farewell party for Bob. He ordered food and drink to be specially prepared and brought up to the loft room for the occasion. Mark West said that about fifteen or so people attended the party and that it was a warm and happy event. At the end, when Bob was preparing to leave and was saying goodbye, Nisargadatta threw his arms around Bob and hugged him, and held him and wept. Bob was extremely moved and was also crying. Nisargadatta clearly loved Bob and Bob loved him.

"I flew home to Australia at the end of March 'seventy-seven. I could have stayed with Nisargadatta, but what more could I get? He was very compassionate and I couldn't help but love the man, you know. People often ask me if Nisargadatta told me to speak and I say, 'No he didn't, there was no special instruction.' And yet it wouldn't have mattered if he'd told me not to speak, he simply couldn't have stopped me. When I first began speaking, what I was saying was a bit rough and garbled – however, it didn't matter, it just had to come out."

## Returning to Australia

On his return to Melbourne in 1977, Bob resumed his job as a security watchman on the waterfront. Much of it was shift work and the money was very good. No one had ever been able to return to this job after they left, but he'd been given a letter before going to India recommending that if he came back he should be given his old job again. The work involved patrolling the wharf area, a potentially dangerous occupation given the threat of break-ins by organised criminal gangs at this time.

The image of a uniformed burly night watchman sitting alone by the warmth of a brazier on a dark wharf on the Melbourne waterfront couldn't be further away from any clichéd notion of *spiritual*. Nisargadatta called the understanding the "natural state"; that pristine awareness in which everything is appearing. This understanding is not predicated upon being anything. It just *is*. A street vendor selling cigarettes in crowded Bombay, a holy man bathing in the Ganges, a night watchman on the Melbourne waterfront – the form is irrelevant. Understanding is all.

Bob was invited to speak at a satsang at the Siddha Yoga ashram in Melbourne but they didn't really warm to what he had to say. He thought that there might have been some interest, but he says that they were too committed to their beliefs to really hear what he was saying. He was keen to share his understanding with those who had helped him in the past. In an attempt to ease the psychological suffering of an old AA member who had looked after him years before, Bob tried to point out how the mental suffering could be alleviated. There was no listening and the old chap died in misery, desperately looking for some sort of purpose and meaning to life. Many people come to Bob looking for a purpose, yet the notion is futile and is illustrated by the story he tells about the dung beetle.

"The dung beetle rolls up a tiny ball of elephant dung and lays its larvae in it. Then it digs a hole about a metre deep in the earth, buries the dung ball and the exhausted beetle dies. When the wet season comes, the earth is softened and the little buried larvae feed on the dung and begin to develop into pupae. They continue to mature into beetles and burrow up to the surface to fly off to where they innately sense the elephants to be.

"One year there is a drought and when some of the beetles fly off there are no elephants to be found, so they die. Other beetles fly off in a different direction where numerous birds and other predators feed on them. The honey badger can smell the presence of the larvae a metre below the surface and it will dig down to eat the young dung beetles even before they surface."

In unpacking the story, Bob asks, "So what is the purpose behind all of this? Is the beetle's function just to lay eggs? Are the larvae merely food for a predator? Is the purpose of the elephant just to shit and provide somewhere for the young dung beetles to grow? Is the purpose of the food that the elephants eat, just to make shit? So you see, the notion of purpose is futile. To say there is purpose requires measuring it from some location. You have to set up a reference point. Without a reference point what can you say?"

For a growing number of people there was a resonance with what he was talking about. Also, the circumstances in his life at that time provided an opportunity to be available for them. "I wasn't back here long before Barbara and I split up again and we sold the house we had in Ivanhoe. Barbara bought a place in Hawthorn and I moved into a little flat in West Melbourne. I was living in the flat for about 18 months and one Saturday afternoon, for something to do, I went along to an AA meeting. Some of the people there remembered me and asked me to speak. After I spoke, somebody came up and said, 'I like what you said, and I want what you've got.'

"At another meeting, there was an Irish fellow pounding on the floor, sick of the world and everybody in it. In the course of his talking he said that he had been trying to find himself. I went up to him after the meeting and asked, 'Do you really want to find yourself?' He said, 'Yes.' So I started talking this stuff to him and amazingly enough, he was open to it. We began to get together regularly and then others began to join in also. This is when I began speaking to groups."

*Top:* Bob with *Flicka* the deer at Alinta Farm

*Bottom:* Bob at Alinta Farm leading *Linta* the German Shepherd on one of the Shetland ponies

## Alinta Farm

"In 1980 somehow or other Barbara and I got back together again and decided to move to the country and buy a farm. It was going to be semi-retirement and we thought we'd have a few animals, grow a few veggies, and you know the story – live off the fat of the land and take it quietly. It didn't work out that way.

"The farm was up on the Murray River near the Barmah forest on the New South Wales side of the border. It was flood country but we didn't realise that at the time. There was a drought the first year, a flood the next year, another drought the following year and another flood the year after that. Things were tough and we had to get rid of much of the animal stock.

"On top of that, I caught Ross River Fever, which is a virus transmitted by infected mosquitoes. Very little was understood about the illness and there was no cure for the condition. It hit me badly and the illness left me debilitated for a long period of time. I could hardly move my body and there was constant exhaustion and pain. Once that would have had me a psychological wreck and probably wanting to end it all.

"Yet throughout that time there was a clear sense that it was okay and that everything would be all right. An underlying sense of wellbeing was constantly there throughout all the difficulties. While there'd be thinking and wondering about what was going to happen, there was no building up of a story about it or getting caught in any sort of mental anguish."

The farm was a little isolated, yet after a while there were a few neighbours sometimes dropping in to talk. People from Melbourne who wanted to talk with Bob would sometimes drive the three-hour journey and Barbara would prepare a room for them to stay over. Bob recounts a conversation with someone full of despair and ringing from a public telephone box in Melbourne. The caller had been talking to Bob for quite a long time. Bob pointed out to him that there is no "I" to do anything and that there is no-one in control of what is happening. The chap responded, "Well that's it then. I won't do anything." Bob replied, "Ok then, just try staying in the phone box." "It was obvious that something would eventually move him out of the box."

With Bob's ongoing health problem, it became a battle to look after the outside work and care for the livestock. When they decided to sell most of the stock, Bob and Barbara had to find another way of earning a living. The 710-acre farm comprised a substantial mud-brick home adjoining a small lake, as well as pasture and bushland. Barbara came up with the idea of turning the property into a tourist farm, a fairly novel idea at that time. The tourist office in nearby Echuca was pleased to have somewhere to direct visitors.

A journalist from Melbourne who had been around Muktananda during the 1974 Melbourne tour arrived to write about Echuca for a Melbourne newspaper. He happened to recognise the Adamson name, drove out to their farm and wrote a feature story on Alinta Tourist Farm. The publicity helped the business grow and there were visitors from interstate and a few from overseas.

There were all sorts of animals to look after on the farm, including peacocks, pheasants, guinea pigs, goats, sheep, cattle, fowl, a piglet named Clementine and a fox called Peter. Bob, being good with animals, had patiently trained their German shepherd to climb up a ladder and onto the house roof. This used to amuse the visitors. The farm was especially exciting for young visitors who had an opportunity to learn about the different aspects of farm life, take rides on the ponies and help Bob feed the animals.

Barbara prepared and served light meals and afternoon teas and took people on tours through the house to view her antiques collection. They ran tours of the farm, accommodated houseguests and catered for some of the bus tours. When a television series depicting 19th century life in the river port of Echuca was being filmed, Bob responded to an advertisement wanting "men with beards" as extras for the film. Casting liked his bushy beard and ironically he was given the role of the town drunk and then some other parts.

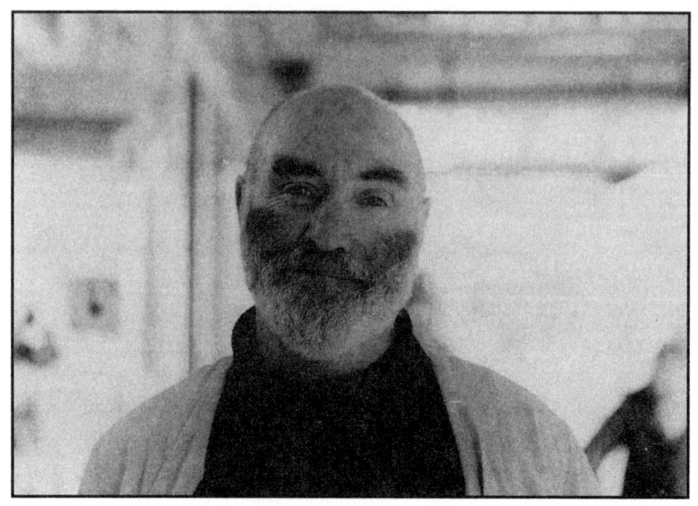

Bob outside the health food shop in Hawthorn, 1985

## Health food shops

Bob's health continued to deteriorate and in 1984 he and Barbara sold Alinta Farm and returned to Melbourne. Medical opinion said there was no cure for the ongoing pain and chronic fatigue Bob experienced as a result of the Ross River Fever. Bob was unwilling to accept the prognosis and set to work researching possible cures and remedies. By taking various herbs and natural medicines, the lingering after-effects of the disease completely disappeared.

As they needed to work to earn a living, Barbara's brother Dale, who was in the health food industry, suggested to Bob and Barb that they should consider running a health food shop. They thought it was a good idea so bought a small health food shop in South Vermont. Bob said that, to begin with, he had no experience of running a business and no business sense at all. "I thought that it was way out of my league, but when we bought the first shop, I soon picked up running a business. At the time, there weren't too many health food shops around. Most of the big wholesalers and the vitamin companies like Blackmores were very helpful to the retailers and would hold lectures to inform them about their products. It was quite interesting because we were given all the necessary information so we could advise the customers.

"I already had a bit of an idea about health foods, herbs and vitamins because I began looking into nutrition when I got sober many years before. Back then I went on a 'get fit' kick and began going to the gym. I started to eat properly and began reading up on wholefoods and diet, so moving into the health food business drew on a long held interest." Barbara also had an interest in health and nutrition and with her background in business they were a good team.

The health food shop went well and later on there was the opportunity to purchase a larger one in Glenferrie Road, Hawthorn. During the week they lived in the flat above the Hawthorn shop which they had renovated and on weekends travelled back to their mountain home at Kalorama in the Dandenong Ranges. Being a good gardener, Bob added further improvements to the large and very beautiful garden.

During this time Bob had been speaking at the AA meetings and people were seeking him out. "There were a few who would continually come around to the shop and ask questions, or want a bit of advice on this, that and the other," he said. "My work in the shop was being interrupted and I couldn't keep taking time during shop hours to speak with each person. So that led to having meetings once or twice a month in a room above the health food shop in Glenferrie Road and we used to get pretty big roll ups.

"At that time it was mostly Alcoholics Anonymous and Narcotics Anonymous people and the format of the meetings was much the same as it is now. I would give a spiel and people would ask a few questions and we would take it from there. On the weekends people would often drive up to our home in Kalorama in the mountains to talk about their problems. Sometimes there'd be a constant stream of people to feed and look after."

In about 1988, Bob wanted to retire from the shop so he sold his part of the business to their friend Joan and she and Barbara continued running it. Five years later, Barbara retired from the shop, studied Bowen Therapy and set up a practice in the tower room of their home. Bob continues with his interest in natural medicines and is very knowledgeable about the latest research and treatments available.

Bob – 1997

## The Meetings

"About a year after I retired, we bought the unit in Deepdene that we now live in. I had been holding the meetings in the church hall on the corner of Hoddle Street and Victoria Parade in East Melbourne. I would catch the tram to the meetings that were held twice a month and then sit and wait for people to show up. Rain, hail or shine I'd be there. Sometimes there'd be a few people and sometimes there'd be a lot. The meetings ran along the lines of an AA meeting where we'd take up a collection to pay for the rent and a cup of tea.

"When I arrived at the hall one night in about 1995, the door was locked and there were people left waiting outside. I went around and saw the priest to get the key and he said that the rent had not been paid for three months. The chap entrusted in taking up the collection had gone off with the money so I decided that I wasn't going to hold meetings anymore. The group were upset about the situation and called a deputation together requesting that I start them again.

"Barbara suggested we hold them in our home and that's when they commenced here. At that time there weren't a great many coming along. Sometimes there were as few as two or three and other times there'd be nine or ten. They were mainly Narcotics Anonymous and Alcoholics Anonymous people but after a while they started bringing their friends and the numbers grew from there. When the meetings finished, Barbara used to provide supper for everyone."

A very large and beautiful tree grows in Bob's front garden. "There are hundreds of pine cones on that tree," he says, "and each cone contains many, many seeds. When the pine cones mature, they fall to the ground and the seeds are released. Some seeds fall on the road and are run over by cars, while other seeds get washed away by the rain. Birds might eat some seeds and some may happen to settle on fertile soil. Even though not every seed is going to sprout, no one seed is any better than another. The potential is there in each and every one of those seeds. Once a seed is sown, it bears fruit of itself. There is nothing more to do."

Bob has given freely to anyone who has sought help. He frequently drops any plans he may have in order to be with someone in need. Back then there could sometimes be dramatic scenes with those who were trying to break their habits and addictions. Likewise it could get pretty intense during the meetings with yelling matches erupting when someone felt they were being challenged. Arguments between people would sometimes blow up and become pretty heavy. It was all grist for the mill; grains of rice rubbing against and polishing each other.

*Top:* Bob and Kalyani in his garden in Deepdene, December 2009

*Below:* Bob's front door

Bob in the garden at Deepdene, 2009

## Getting More Widely Known

Bob became more widely known after his words first appeared in a booklet put together by Gilbert Schultz. Gilbert had heard about Bob at Ramesh Balsekar's place in Mumbai and on his return to Sydney was given an audiotape of Bob speaking. Gilbert transcribed it and contacted Bob in mid-2000 to ask if he could put it into booklet form. A fortnight later he mailed the completed booklet to Bob and soon afterwards flew to Melbourne to meet him.

Gilbert recounts, "I was puzzled by Bob because he did not play any games of being special. He was so ordinary. It took me quite a while to realise that he was totally genuine. What he shared with everyone was not some philosophical view. He spoke from the immediacy about the immediacy. Every word was uncontrived and an expression of the knowing that he is, not mere theoretical knowledge. No song and dance, no self-image crap that we are used to seeing with teachers and gurus. What he expresses is genuine."

When he asked Bob about doing further transcriptions, Gilbert said, "He unceremoniously handed me thirty tapes in a plastic shopping bag." The transcribed and edited material was published the following year as the book *What's Wrong with Right Now Unless You Think About It?* The publication brought a wider audience both nationally and internationally and as a result James Braha invited Bob to come and teach in America. He and Barbara flew to Florida in mid-2004 and stayed for five weeks with the Brahas. People would arrive each day for the talks and discussions, which went on from morning until night. Then over the following three weeks, Bob gave talks in Connecticut, Chicago and Santa Cruz.

John Wheeler met Bob in Melbourne in 2003 and transcribed further material for the second book *Presence-Awareness*. This was followed by James Braha's book *Living Reality*, which recounts his time spent with the Adamsons and is woven around material from the daily talks and question sessions. On the other side of the Atlantic, Bob gave talks in Amsterdam and was videoed by a Dutch television station. The programme was well received and is still aired from time to time. Since then there have been further publications, a website, CDs and DVDs, interviews on the internet, and his words have been translated into several other languages.

## The Message, Not the Messenger.

Bob sometimes tells a story that I first heard in 1974. It is about an earnest spiritual seeker who went to a guru in order to find the truth. The seeker arrived at the ashram and was told he would need to serve the guru for twelve years in order to attain enlightenment. He carried out his *seva* diligently, ate only pure foods, recited the sacred texts, chanted the holy names of God, focused the mantra with his breath, learned to meditate with a silent mind, experienced ecstatic and visionary states and, most importantly, worshipped the guru.

Every time he saw the guru coming he would fall on his knees and *pranam* to him with great reverence. The guru seemed amused each time he saw him. As the seeker threw himself at his feet, the guru would say to him "That thou art" and walk off.

After twelve years passed, the spiritual seeker had still not found the truth he had been working so hard to find. So he packed his bags and left the ashram to see another guru in a nearby village.

When he arrived, he was taken to meet him and, when questioned, explained that he had served the other guru faithfully for twelve years but had still not found the truth. The guru sat quietly and looked at him for a few moments and then said, "That thou art." This time the seeker heard what was being said with the full understanding of its actuality.

This is the simplicity of what is being pointed to. It is the same message the ancients speak of and which has been handed down through the ages. Yet the mind has a curious habit of fixating on the messenger and overlooking the message. In this way it avoids its own demise. While the attention is focused on the messenger, "That thou art" simply remains a catchphrase.

There is nothing to get and no one to attain anything. Any attempt to understand with the mind simply keeps the conceptual mind-stream flowing. Thinking busies itself trying to attain the goal of non-thinking; it behaves like a rodent in a wheel. It aims for a notion of *an understanding* it is imagining. It is a thought trying to take hold of another thought – an impossibility.

Nisargadatta said, "Do not struggle to come out of the mud of your own concepts, you will only go deeper. Remain still." You cannot think your way out. It is unresolvable. In remaining still and stopping the chatter, simply put a STOP on the thought flow, simply pause a thought.

In the words of Huang Po, "Understanding comes through an inexpressible mystery. The approach is called *The Gateway to Stillness beyond all Activity.* Know that a *sudden comprehension* arises, when the clutter of conceptual thinking and discriminating thought activity subsides."

The Dzogchen Buddhists call it *The Great Perfection* or non-conceptual awareness; the emptiness before thoughts appear and start believing in themselves. Pristine and original. Omnipresence, omnipotence, omniscience. Singularity undivided by thought. One without a second. Not even one… simply *That*.

In the stillness, the emptiness, the oneness… taste the ineffable, the eternal, the sublime and all pervading essence. Recognise that is what you are.

PART 2

# The Teaching

Extracts from Talks, Question and Answer Sessions and Interviews

## Not Just for the Few

**Bob:** Have you all left your self-centres at the door? It makes it much easier if you do. Most of you in the room have been here before, so you've got a good idea of what it's all about. We say that this understanding is not just for the few, it's everybody's right because it's based on pure simplicity itself – oneness. Although it's been put around that it's very hard to obtain, there is actually nothing simpler than one. This understanding has been handed down through the centuries – far back before any documentation. It had been known only to a few and the reason was that communities were fairly isolated and the means of communication were limited. So there'd only be a few who'd hear about it from someone in a village somewhere.

Not everybody wants to look at this stuff and that does not matter. That's the way they are patterning and the way they're functioning. Yet whether they look at it or not, they are *That*. What you are seeking, you already are. The great word or *Mahavakya* is *I am That*, this is *That*, everything is *That*.

But what is this *That* which they're talking about? It's something that cannot be conceptualised. You can't put a word or a label on it. Over the centuries there have been a lot of good pointers. One of the Buddhist ones is *cognising emptiness*. It is emptiness, no-thing; it's not a vacuum or a void – it's suffused with knowing. In other words, suffused with intelligence – the activity of knowing. That's why I sometimes use the concept, "intelligence energy".

I'm talking about the same intelligence that functions as this universe. If you have a look out there in space, you'll see the planets moving around, galaxies forming and breaking down, earth orbiting the sun, tides coming in and out, seasons coming and going. For all these things to be happening implies it's suffused with an innate intelligence.

There are many metaphors for that oneness. They call it space-like awareness, cognising emptiness, pure awareness, consciousness. The Buddhists again in the Dzogchen scriptures say it's non-conceptual, ever-fresh, self-shining, presence awareness, just this and nothing else. If you look at that closely, that's a very accurate description of you, right here, right now. Without any concepts, you are seeing and knowing. Can you say the seeing, the knowing, hearing or functioning has any beginning? Can you say it has any ending? Can you point to where you start seeing or where you end seeing, or hearing? So it's ever-fresh, self-shining, self-knowing. You don't need another self to try to find yourself. That would be an impossibility. We have created this false sense of self and then we go looking from that point of view to try to find out what we really are. Yet that self-knowing is constantly with us.

And you cannot negate your presence. Nobody can say, *I am not*. Each one of us knows that *I am*. But it's not that thought, *I am* that we're talking about, that's simply the way it's translating through the mind. That sense of presence, the awareness of presence, translates through the thought, *I am*. So you're there before the thought. When you look and investigate you'll find you're not the body, nor the mind. The body-mind is just another pattern or appearance in this emptiness, just as the tree, the flower, the cloud and everything else is.

So the intelligence energy that functions as the universe is the activity of knowing. Before we can say, "I know this, or I know that", there is that naked knowingness, or naked intelligence, or naked awareness, before it's translated into any concept. And because that I-N-G is on the knowing – it's not just know, the knower or the known, it's know-ing. That I-N-G implies that it's something that's actively taking place in the immediacy of this moment. We call it a moment, but it's not even that.

When did you start knowing? Have you finished knowing? It is going on naturally before you start discriminating with the mind and saying *I know this*, or *I don't know that*. You can't negate the knowing. It's an activity that's happening right now. And what is an activity? An activity is a movement of energy? So again, intelligence energy – the activity of knowing.

None of these terms can ever get anywhere near it. That's why they tell us in the Gita, *the sword can't cut it, the fire can't burn it, the wind can't dry it, the water can't drown it* – purely and simply because it contains all of those things. None of those things could *be* without it. So how can you grasp it with a concept when it contains all concepts? We can only use terms such as *That,* or awareness. We are talking about the no-thing, the un-manifest. We call this a phenomenal universe – a universe made up of phenomena. These stars and galaxies are all phenomena. And the definition of phenomena is that which *appears to be.*

Now the opposite of phenomenon is the *noumenon* which means the un-manifest, the emptiness. The dictionary definition of *noumenon* is *That which is.* The un-manifest is the actuality, the *what is.* The phenomenon, the patterning universe, is appearance only. Now when we speak about that appearance, we generally exclude ourselves and say that this is appearing to me, or this is my appearance. Yet what we're expressing as, is the appearance.

The very life essence is the indivisible, pure, intelligence energy. It's just been pointed out that it can't be grasped with a concept, and because it is no-thing, it cannot be negated either. You might have read many books, done many practices, done lots of things and heard about many great masters, but not one of them has ever gone beyond nothing, no-thing. With the awareness of being no-thing, you've gone as far as you can ever go; you're there where you've always been. You are that no-thing that's expressing, that is happening as that human shape and form. The expression is happening just as it is patterning and expressing every other shape and form. In the Gita they say... *from Brahma to a clump of grass.* It's all that. That is what you are.

That is why I say that it's everybody's right, and there are some people here who understand that already. Let life unfold from the point of view that what you really are is the unmanifest, the pure essence. 

## The Essence Is the Unmanifest and Has Never Changed

**Q:** *How do I stay in the awareness? It seems like it comes and goes.*

**Bob:** If you think you've got it and then lose it, always come back to what the ancients tell us. They say it's one without a second – you are already that. The thought, *I've lost it,* or *I've got it* is the totality also; it's how it's appearing. Everything becomes all inclusive. Initially, when we're looking at this stuff, we pull it all apart and see that there's no entity there with any substance or any independent nature. And when you see that, you don't have to pull it apart anymore. Whether it's seemingly *got* or seemingly *lost,* everything that is happening is *That.*

**Q:** *And there's no-one who can change that?*

**Bob:** It changes by itself, it alters of itself. As manifestation, it's certain to change because the whole manifestation is transient and is constantly changing – from the furthermost galaxy down to the smallest subatomic particle – it's constantly changing in appearance. But the essence of it is the unmanifest and has never changed. Yet it contains all the changes, and the changes can't contain it, and that's what we try

to do when we try to grasp it with a thought. We try to grasp the unchangeable with a changeable thing. The definition of reality is that which never changes.

**Q:** *I don't know whether I can come to terms with the fact that I don't exist.*

**Bob:** Nobody says anything about non-existence. You are existence itself. There is only one existence, one presence, one power, one intelligence. Instead of confining yourself to that little pattern you call *me,* which in the scheme of things is nothing, you're trying to work it out in the mind. *Me* can never come to terms with it. As Nisargadatta says, "You're trying to grasp it with a concept – and you fail. And you are bound to fail." He means you'll always fail while you're trying to grasp it with a concept.

But, full stop right now, without a thought, are there any concepts going on? Yet have you stopped seeing? Have you stopped hearing? Have you stopped being aware? In that instant without a concept, without a thought, before another concept arises, you realise that you *are* existence; you are the living-ness, the being-ness. Do you have to come to terms with that? You can only come to terms with it with another concept. It's just as it is – unadorned, naked awareness – not adorned by any concepts. As the poem says, "It's closer than your breathing, nearer than your hands and feet." You've never been away from it. Never could.

***Participant:*** *What a true expression: I cannot come to* *terms with this – because the* I *is fighting for its survival. That limited identity we think we are is just so invested and it thinks that if it disappears then the whole show will fall to bits. Yet the identity has no reality and, with that understanding and the attention withdrawn, then it simply dissolves. What appears is what's already here, always was and always is.*

**Bob:** Remember that this is the actuality. Nobody can live a moment ago. That's gone. It's finished. You can recall it, but when you're recalling it, the only actuality it's got is what you're giving it in this moment. Nobody can live a moment in the future. You can anticipate and imagine the future, but you can't live the future. If you're not recalling the past, nor imagining or anticipating the future, where does that leave you?

It leaves you here, in this presence awareness, which is clear and empty. It's never been contaminated or hurt by any of the dramas or trials that have gone on in the mind. That living essence has never been touched. It's the one essence. It has never changed its true nature.

## Who is Asking the Question?

**Q:** *I'm just wondering whether you could run through the inquiry?*

**Bob:** What's the question you're supposed to ask?

**Q:** *Who am I?*

**Bob:** Well, have you ever found out, who am I?

**Q:** *No.*

**Bob:** Instead of asking, "Who am I?" ask yourself, "Who is asking the question, 'Who am I?' Who is this questioner who is asking, 'Who am I?'"

**Q:** *Mm.*

**Bob**: What do you realise from that?

**Q:** *I'd say that it is the mind, thought.*

**Bob:** All right, the mind or thought is the questioner. So the mind or thought is asking, who is the questioner asking the question? The mind or thought is the questioner. Is that right?

**Q:** *Yes.*

**Bob**: Well what's the question?

**Q:** *Who am I?*

**Bob:** What is that?

**Q:** *It's a thought.*

**Bob:** Yes, a concept, a thought. The questioner, which is a thought or a concept, is the question itself, which is a thought or a concept. There is no difference between them. So if there's no questioner, there can't be a question. Where does that leave you – without a question or a questioner?

**Q:** *So if there's no questioner, there can't be a question?*

**Bob:** With neither a question nor a questioner, where does that leave you?

**Q:** *It would be nothing.*

Bob: So you're the bearer of a thought, the bearer of a concept. Cancel out the questioner and the question and there is a naked awareness. You've found out, who am I? Instead of asking the question and mulling it over in your mind for years and years, getting nowhere, see that the questioner is the question itself. People talk about being prior to the mind and do all sorts of antics trying to get there. The questioner can't be anything other than the question. They both cancel each other out. No question, no questioner. Without a question, or a questioner, I haven't disappeared or fallen apart. That moment you're prior to the mind, and gone beyond thought. So beyond thought, you must be prior to thought. And that's the simplicity of it.

***Participant:*** *That's a nice way of putting it, Bob. You say we're bearers of thoughts and questions, but when those thoughts and concepts and questions disappear, there's no bearer either, and then we are just present. There is just presence awareness, which is prior to all the stuff that's arising, prior to the appearance. Yet the appearance is it.*

**Bob:** All the pointers will take you home if you look into them.

## Undistracted Non-Meditation

**Q:** *I've just come out of a ten-day meditation retreat. What I was experiencing was confusion with what I know.*

**Bob:** Do you know what you're not?

**Q:** *Yes.*

**Bob:** What are you not?

**Q:** *I'm not my mind, or my thoughts, or my body.*

**Bob:** That's right. So who would need to meditate if you're not your mind, your thoughts, your body, and what is there to meditate on?

**Q:** *Yes, and this is the conflict. I'm realising it's all coming from me, the meditator, the watcher, me the one who needs mental purification.*

**Bob:** So that's subtly keeping the idea of a separate entity going, isn't it?

**Q:** *Yes.*

**Bob:** There's a trying there.

**Q:** *Yes, there's an effort.*

**Bob:** In the Dzogchen, the ultimate Buddhist teachings, they call it undistracted, non-meditation. The very idea of meditating is distracting you from non-meditation, so you are back in trouble. (*Laughing*) Undistracted non-meditation is going on all the time, when there's no-one to meditate, and nothing to meditate on. That is the natural meditation and that is what you are.

**Q:** *Yes, but I did get a lot out of it.*

**Bob:** Yes, you get a lot out of it, but then you'll go back to another one to get a lot more out of it. (*Laughing*) And so it goes on. People have been doing these practices for 10, 20, 30 years, and have never found the answer there. I did all these practices, and you think you must be getting close. But you realise that if you're looking at something for so long and looking in the mind, it might dawn on you that maybe you're looking in the wrong direction.

And then you may say, what direction, what way is there outside of the mind? Whichever way you go is always in the mind – north, south, and east, west, high or low – it's always in the mind. There is only one way out of the mind. Full stop. When you full stop, you pause a thought in that moment, don't you? And before another thought has arisen, what's happening? Pause a thought right now? Just repeat a word. Repeat it out loud. Any word.

**Q:** *Flower.*

**Bob:** Repeat it and keep going.

**Q:** *Flower, flower, flower, flower, flower....*

**Bob:** Stop. (*Holds up his hand*) Now in that stopping, the word was only a thought expressed loudly, wasn't it?

**Q:** *Yes.*

**Bob:** In that stopping, did you stop seeing? Did you stop being aware? In that split moment you were in non-conceptual awareness, pure emptiness. The functioning was happening, prior to any entity there thinking. Now that gives you a taste of your true nature – the non-conceptual awareness. It's easy enough to get to. Now in that pause, before another thought arose, there is just that naked awareness. When there are no concepts there and that bare awareness is there, what happened? Another concept might arise and then the thinking might start.

Realise that they all happen on that naked awareness that is constantly there. Everything is happening in that, so that's what you actually are. The thoughts come and go. They can be paused and the feelings and emotions can all be paused. But the essence on which they appear has no beginning and has no ending. You'll never find the answer in the mind so it's pointless looking there. When you realise that, you stop looking there.

**Q:** *Yes.*

**Bob:** You are *That.*

**Q:** *Yes, I am* That.

**Bob:** Don't forget it.

## I'm Speaking to That I Am, That I Am

**Bob:** The search itself is the problem. While you are seeking, there is a belief that there's something you don't have right now but will get at some future time if you do certain things. If you've got that belief, you're caught up in the mental concept of time and have seemingly moved away from the immediacy, from omnipresence.

The *Mahavakya* or what they call the Great Word is *I am That, Thou art That, This is That.* When I say, "I am not speaking to any body, I'm not speaking to any mind. I'm speaking to that *I am,* that I am – to that sense of presence that expresses through the mind as the thought *I am.*" It's not the thought *I am,* but that sense of presence, that presence of awareness that you cannot negate. There is a sense of presence with each and every one of you right now in the immediacy of this moment. It's the presence of awareness, or the awareness of presence. Nobody sitting here can say *I am not.* Each one knows *I am.*

So that's what we're speaking to – the sense of presence that is expressing through the mind as the thought and that which is speaking to it. In actuality, it is that sense of presence speaking to itself. There will be a resonance in hearing it. The resonance happens because innately you already know it. You recognise that you are *That* and always have been.

Another thing we say is that you won't find the answer in the mind, so it's pointless looking there. In looking, is there any place that is outside of the mind? Every direction you look in is always in the mind. When you realise that you can't get out of the mind by looking, what must happen? Wouldn't there just be a natural full stop? In that full stop, the thought is paused for a brief moment. In that pause, when there's no thought going on, you haven't stopped seeing, you haven't stopped hearing, you haven't disappeared and you haven't fallen apart. When there's no conceptualising going on, no thinking, you are prior to the mind. And that's how simple it really is.

**Q:** *The veil of duality seems so thick and so prevailing and yet you say that there's no separateness. What is your experience from moment to moment? Do you fluctuate between the awareness of all and then separateness?*

**Bob:** I once believed that I was that separate entity, a separate person, a separate body if you like; then, in seeing and investigating, it became absolutely clear that I wasn't. I can't even function from the idea that there is anything that could possibly be separate. You say that the veil of duality is so thick; well, when you look, it's not. You see, we miss the simplicity of what is immediate. It's not a matter of going in and out of awareness – awareness is all there is and that is what you truly are. You are that awareness and you can never fall out of it. You don't have to search for it. Just try and get away from it, try and not be aware.

You say that there are times when you don't see it, but when recalled, you realise that you didn't disappear; you didn't fall apart when you weren't remembering. To be able to say that it wasn't seen or wasn't there for a while, what has that taken place on? Nothing could have appeared outside of awareness; it is omnipresence.

We'll use the metaphor of the sun in the sky. Even though a cloud might be blocking the sun, the sun hasn't left the sky, has it? There's nothing that could convince you that the sun has disappeared. Realise that it's the sun itself that forms the cloud. The warmth from its shining evaporates water, clouds then form and the warmed air causes the wind to stir. The cloud is not attached to the sky so it gets blown away. In turn, the clouds condense and fall as rain. Yet the sun hasn't done anything but shine and clouds have formed.

It is the same with the awareness that you are. It is self-shining. There can be a cloud of thoughts seemingly blocking the awareness but that awareness has not gone away. There's no thought that has ever attached to the mind either. No thought has ever been stuck there; the thoughts simply come and go. We, however, fixate on them in the belief that we are an entity. It is the "I" thought fixating on another thought. So thought is always fighting with thought, resisting thought. And that is conflict and our sense of separation.

**Q:** *It seems that wanting to get something else creates the suffering.*

**Bob:** Yes. There's nothing else to get. You are already *That*.

## Everything Is Perfectly Resolved

***Participant:*** *The fact is, this* I *has no reality and no substance whatsoever. I'd spent years and years working on it, attempting to transcend the ego and doing so many different practices endlessly. Then the blinding flash of the obvious was that once it's truly understood that the* I *has no independent existence except that which is vested in it, and in seeing through that – all that happens is an uncovering. That veil, that fantasy, is only held together by a belief in it. And it's amazing how easy it is to miss that.*

**Bob:** And that's the key to the whole lot. That sense of separation first came upon us in the belief of an *I*, that sense of a *me*. So get that, and the whole lot dissolves. The belief that there is a separate entity is erroneous.

**Q***: So could the function of the mind wanting to label things be to stop you from seeing the truth? Is that what its function is?*

**Bob:** No. The mind is a very useful instrument when it's utilised. This building was an idea in somebody's mind once, and the pictures on the wall were an idea, the technology was an idea, the music, the art, the capacity for reading, it's all happening through this human form, this human pattern. It's a vibration. So when it vibrates to the other extreme and says, "I'm not good enough, I can't do this, I've got low self-esteem, people don't like me", it becomes self-destructive. We take ourselves to be that entity without questioning it. But if it's left alone, what happens? You're open to the universe and God knows what talents are likely to come out. Amazing things that have been discovered have all come through the mind. So it's a useful instrument when it's understood.

**Q**: *So it's a dysfunctional instrument when it's not used properly?*

**Bob**: That's right, it's self-destructive. It's the cause of all our problems, all of our psychological suffering. *Me* is the cause of my fear, my anxiety, my resentment, my self-pity, and all of these problems are the effects. That's what so-called karma is – cause and effect. Yet what happens when I see that the cause is a fiction and I ask myself the simple question, "Can there be an effect without a cause?" You don't have to work on the effect; just see that if they're not attributed to an entity, a cause, then where are they going to lodge? They've got nowhere to fixate so they just move on. They'll still come up, but they don't hang around. They may play around for a while and might even be useful in the functioning.

A bit of anger now and again may get something moving or get you through some situation. But it doesn't hang around and get stuck and beat us up. We beat ourselves up with the word. If somebody gives you a thumping out in the street then as soon as you walk away, you start to slowly recover. But if somebody calls you names, you carry it around for weeks and it eats you up. And we're beating ourselves up all the time with the labels we put on ourselves.

Bankei was a Zen Buddhist monk who for many years sat meditating on hard rocks. His backside was raw and ulcerated and he became seriously ill. He was near death when it suddenly dawned on him that everything is perfectly resolved in the unborn Buddha mind and his search ended. He then realised, "Why exchange the Unborn Buddha mind for thought?" Bankei regained his health and travelled around the country talking to the thousands of people who used to come to listen to his addresses.

What he was saying was so simple. Everything is perfectly resolved in the unborn Buddha mind. The unborn mind he is talking about is what is before thought arises. This universe resolves itself. There's nothing out there pulling the strings. From our limited point of view it can seem a chaotic universe. But if you look at the overall picture, it's very orderly. Yet what we continually do is exchange that unborn, natural mind for thought and try to conceptualise our way out.

Everything's perfectly resolved in the unborn mind so why exchange it for thought? Are you going to exchange that Buddha mind for thought? Or are you going to disregard the concepts, not take any vested interest in them, or place any fixation on them? Let them be. And let the unborn resolve itself.

It brought you into existence with no entity doing that. And it's lived as this pattern of energy, even though at one stage it believed it was doing all the living. It got itself into a hell of a lot of strife and that's the way it happened anyway. It turned it around to see and understand the actuality of what's going on here. It's the unborn – not Bob – that did anything about it.

***Participant:*** *I've found a sense of non-locality, the freedom of not being anywhere in particular.*

**Bob:** Can emptiness be in one particular spot? Can space be in a particular spot or is it more pervasive? What locality has space got?

**Q:** *So is space a concept?*

**Bob:** Yes. (*Laughing*) Any term you use is a concept. You can't say what you are. You can negate any concepts you'd like to put on it, but you can't negate your being-ness, can you?

**Q:** *No.*

**Bob:** You can't say, *I am not.* In the very saying of it, there must be that knowing that there is something there that's enabling it to be said. And what is it?

**Q:** *That.*

**Bob:** Exactly. And that is what you are. The great word is *I am That.*

***Participant:*** *And no matter what we conceptualise, whatever you perceive is not it.*

**Q:** *There is always perception isn't there?*

**Bob:** Perceiving is happening, but when you give it a point and say *I'm perceiving,* you've created a pseudo subject. I'm perceiving this or I'm perceiving that has created an object, and there is the seeming subject/ object split. The actuality is the functioning that's happening naturally – the seeing, hearing, tasting, touching, smelling.

## Thinking, Feeling and Emotion

**Bob:** Thought, feeling and emotion are one and the same thing, just as steam, water and ice are basically one and the same. You can't burst into tears right now. First a sad thought might arise and if you keep it there long enough, then a sad feeling will well up in you. Keep that sad feeling there long enough and the tears will come. Now we've done this so many times, we've sort of hypnotised ourselves. We see something and before we realise it, the thoughts and the emotions can be there almost instantly. Then we divide them up and we try working on our emotions, our feelings and all the rest of it. In that division it keeps on going forever.

At the time when you label the emotion as fear, it's just a sensation. It's not called *fear* until you label it. You then relate it to past events that you've labelled as fear. As soon as you do that you've added all the other fears to it and those feelings and sensations come up. You are not going to be *feeling-less* or *emotion-less,* but when they come up, they are seen as they are in the moment. They are not related to past events and experiences, and they're not a problem.

Watch what happens in nature. The lion will take off after a herd of antelope. Some of the antelope might have been lying down, but they get up and run off straight away. After the lion has caught one antelope, the rest will then get on with living again and eating. If the lion chased us, we'd be looking over our shoulder for the rest of the day saying "Shit, where is he now? Is he still coming?" We'd carry the fear around and beat ourselves up with it, even though the danger had long since past.

**Q:** *So how do you get rid of all the emotions that we've labelled?*

**Bob:** Well, again, have a look at it. What conditioning is there right now if you don't think about it? All it is is an expression of that pure intelligence energy. Take the label and the meaning out of it and it's just another movement of energy. The feelings and sensations are movements of energy.

**Q:** *The experiencing of the body feels so predominant. It feels like there is an entity.*

**Bob**: Yeah, it makes it feel like it, but have a look and see if you can find anything. It's just a feeling or a sensation which you say feels like an entity. But you see, what you're trying to do is to take it back to the no-thing conceptually. You are trying to grasp it with a concept – maybe it's this, or maybe it's that. That's what we've been doing all our lives. If you have not found the answer there, do you think you're going to find it now? Do you think one day maybe you will find a conceptual answer to say, "This is what I am" – when a concept is only a mental construct. You are not an appearance. You are the reality, and the reality that you are is *no-thing*. The definition of reality is *That* which never changes. It's the so-called emptiness, or the no-thing that never changes. What can you add to no-thing? What can you take away from no-thing?

## The Ego Is Fiction

Our problems arise from the idea of a separate entity, a *me* that we learn at about the age of two or two and a half years. What can you do with the word, *me* or *I*? You can't do much with it. So what we do is add events, experiences and conditioning – the things that have happened to us. The energy of belief goes into that and it seemingly concretises. It seems to become real. And that's what we call the self-centre or the ego. It becomes the reference point that I believe myself to be. Something comes up and I like it. How would I know I liked it? Well if something's happened previously and I'm relating it to a past image, I say, "This is good."

Then what happens when the good things tend to move away after a while, and I don't want them to go? When I really like them, what do I do? I try to resist them going, and what is resistance? Resistance is conflict, and conflict is dis-ease. If you're in conflict, you're uneasy – not at ease. That's disease. If something comes up and I don't like it, I'm referring to this *me* of memory again, and if I don't like it, what do I do? I try to push it away and get rid of it. Again, there is resistance, conflict and dis-ease.

In nature, the pairs of opposites are constantly functioning and there couldn't be any dualism without that constant functioning of the opposites. These opposites are not in conflict with one another. There is nothing taking a stance against the other. If it is spring now, soon it will be summer. Spring's not saying, "I wish it were summer." It moves on naturally, without any conflict. The incoming tide doesn't fight the outgoing tide. A storm will come through and blow things apart. After a while it dissipates and nature gradually renews itself. The pairs of opposites are constantly there, but there is no conflict.

With us, the pairs of opposites are constantly in conflict because we're constantly relating or referring to this mental image of the way we think or believe things should be; not leaving things as they are, but wanting them to be the way we think they should be. So, all our problems are really problems of relationship – not just the male-female relationship. Problems are problems of relationship – *relative to,* and it's always relative to this self-image we've got. When you see it's a fictitious image based on past events and past experience, you see the trap we put ourselves in.

And you'll hear that in the great traditions, too. They'll tell you the same thing. It's selfishness, self-centredness and self-will that are the problem. They say you have to sublimate this ego and destroy it. You have to do all sorts of things with it, and in that struggle to do that, what happens? What are you doing it with? It's the ego fighting against the ego. Have a look at it closely and you'll see that the ego is a fiction. It never existed. It never could.

It can be pointed out quite simply right now. Everybody is seeing right now. You're seeing quite effortlessly. The seeing is going on. Everybody is also hearing right now. The seeing is happening, the hearing is happening. Ask yourself, "Is my eye telling me I see?" Well my eye is not saying, "Look at this, Bob, or look at that." The seeing is happening through the eye, but it's translated by the thought, *I see;* I see this, I see that.

The hearing is happening through the ear. The ear is not telling me, *I hear.* Again it's translated by the thought, *I hear.* So the eye is not telling me *I see* and the ear is not telling me *I hear,* but the thought comes up and translates it. Now ask yourself this: can the thought, *I see,* actually see? Look closely and you'll realise that the thought is not seeing. Can the thought, *I hear,* actually do the hearing? All the thought is doing is translating. This ego is thought up and has no power to see, to hear or to be aware. The thought, *I choose,* can't choose. The thought, *I'm aware,* is not your awareness.

So this fictitious ego is an idea to which we have been in bondage for all these years. The belief that it is an entity that can choose, has self-will, self-awareness, is having bad luck, etc, is just a thought. In the seeing that it's a fiction, what's going to happen then? Isn't the natural livingness going to carry on the way it's been carrying on anyway? It's breathing you, it's beating your heart, it's growing your hair and fingernails, digesting your food, replacing cells, causing the thinking, feelings, emotions and everything to happen quite effortlessly.

If all of the functioning is not being related to a *me,* then what's the problem? Is good or bad a problem unless it's related to an entity that thinks it should be some other way? It doesn't mean to say problems won't come up. They'll come up, sure, because as in nature, the pairs of opposites are constantly functioning, but when they are coming up, they are seen for what they are. With un-fixated awareness, they move on. When we're fixating on something, clinging to something, attaching to something, it keeps it there. There's a resistance going on and it's not free to move.

That's why we say that all our problems come from the belief in a separate entity. See that it was never real and you realise things have just happened that way.

**Q:** *The ego seems to be an extraordinary construction – a notion, a kind of bundle of ideas?*

**Bob:** It's uncreated. It's all so-called mind stuff. And all "mind" is, is thought. The Buddhists call it *all minds*. They're not discriminating between mind and awareness. It's all mind in their point of view – all consciousness. That natural innate knowing-ness is there – it's not born, doesn't have any beginning, doesn't have any end. It's not bound by time and it can't be grasped from any point because there's no point, no centre and no circumference to it. It just is.

**Q:** *You link thoughts, feelings and emotion together and say they are the same thing?*

**Bob:** And what's emotion about? Isn't it about the image being affected by the thought? If thought hangs around long enough it becomes feeling. Then if feeling hangs around, it becomes emotion. It moves from subtle thought into feeling then emotion. It's one and the same thing really – it stirs up this body pattern which is just another form of energy. To a certain extent, you need the thoughts, feelings and emotions to function. But when we're bound into them so that we believe it, then it becomes self-destructive. That's all time – mind is the past, mind is time. Mind is all these things. It's all mind stuff....

**Q:** *What you seem to say is that when you understand that the construction, the reference point, identity, ego – call it what you like – is not real, then a dissolution happens and you fall into the seeing.*

**Bob:** It's un-fixated awareness, where it's not fixating on the no-thing or anything else. It's just free in the immediacy of the moment to go whichever way it goes. And if it latches onto something, that's not fixated on either. If it goes back in the other direction, it's not fixated on either.

**Q:** *So you say that reference points come and reference points go.*

**Bob:** Everything comes and everything goes. Choices are made – no choice maker. No reference point holder. The preferences may come up – no preference holder. These labels could all come up, you know. So it's all there and it's really always free to move in whatever direction it likes.

**Q:** *So it dissipates because it's seen for what it is?*

**Bob:** Yes, it's recognised again for what it is. It's the thinking or conceptualising that is the only problem we've ever had. But it needn't be a problem if it's understood. And that's what the ancients point out. There is nothing either good or bad, but the thinking makes it so... and nothing can trouble you except your own imagination.

**Q:** *There seems to be an expectation that stopping the thinking would halt the pain?*

**Bob:** Nothing wrong with thinking. But if it is divided into a thinker and a thought, then it's problematic. There's nothing wrong with experiencing. When it's divided into an experience – this experience and that experience – it becomes a problem. It's the mental division that causes the problem. There is nothing wrong with seeing. In the seer and the seen, the division is only conceptual. It's just made up of concepts, thoughts and ideas. I see this, that and the other, whatever you're seeing – is a label you've got for what you're seeing. And so it's a thought always in conflict with a thought... and there's resistance to it all. If it's understood that the two are both ends of the same stick, then it really doesn't matter.

## Thinking Is Appearing Just Like Everything Else

**Q:** *So the chatter, the thinking that we focus on, clouds the actuality that we are?*

**Bob:** If there is not a focusing on the thinking, then it is just appearing like everything else. Is that underlying essence being obscured by the thoughts? If it is left as the activity of thinking, then it's just appearing like everything else. So is anything being obscured?

**Q:** *How do we stop the thinking? It seems to run like traffic.*

**Bob:** Is there any need to stop the thinking if it is realised what it is taking place in? What are the clouds taking place in? Isn't the cloud in space? Do you have to stop the cloud to recognise the space, or do you realise that the space is always and ever the background in which the clouds appear? It's not a matter of trying to stop the thinking – it is simply understanding what you actually are. You are that essence itself, not the concepts or anything that appears on it.

**Q:** *So there is not a problem with thinking? It's the thought of a separate* me *with a sense of volition doing the thinking that creates the issues?*

**Bob:** Isn't it all another group of thoughts thinking that it's *me*? It's the believed-in thought-entity that is the problem. When you realise that thinking, like everything else, is just happening, there's no thinker and there's no entity there at all. Could there be a problem if it's not discriminated or divided in any way, shape or form? It's purely *what is*, non-dual.

**Q:** *Nisargadatta said, "You must not go back, undo, uproot, abandon the conquered ground. Tenacity of purpose in pursuit will bring you to your goal." It seems that a supreme effort is required.*

**Bob:** He also said, "When effort is needed, effort will take place." Insight or experience is conquered ground. Instead of going on with the next insight, we go back trying to get something that was similar to that last experience. It is the freshness and newness enabling expressions or experiences to appear and not be compromised by any comparison to a previous one. In the *Hsin Hsin Ming* it states, "Make the smallest distinction, however, and heaven and earth are set infinitely apart."

## The Reference Point Is the Cause of All My Problems

**Q:** *It seems like I have a subtle belief that I'm going to get something. So who is it that wants to get it?*

**Bob:** Everything is relative to that self-centre or ego. It's judged from there as good or bad, pleasant or unpleasant. You've experienced something before so you go back into memory and say that wasn't too good so it will be the same this time. Instead of seeing things fresh in the moment, they are referred to the image we have of ourselves and it's always relative to that image. So our problem is a problem of relativity, relationship, relative to. All problems are problems of relationship. So when you've got this male/female relationship, no wonder you're always in strife. There's no relationship – just a natural merging, natural coming together, or natural moving away, which is the way nature functions.

We make it a problem because we compare it to the image of what we like and, when it starts to move away, what do we do? We don't want it to move away, so we resist the moving and try to hang on to it. Or, if it's something that comes up and we don't like it, what happens? We want to push it away, so what do we do? We resist it again, resistance is conflict and conflict is disease. No wonder we are unhappy and bound in psychological suffering. If we were able to choose our thoughts, why would we ever have an unhappy one? Why would we ever have an angry thought, or a fearful thought?

So you see it's all problems of relationship to that self-centre. See the resistance; recognise the resistance – that's all you can do. In the recognition, see where you are recognising it from. You must be recognising it from its opposite. If you're totally resistant, you don't realise it. Totally angry, you don't realise it because you're totally absorbed, totally into it. And the recognition of resistance is from the point of non-resistance. At that moment you're out of it. And even if the pattern comes up again out of habit, then recognise again.

You start to get the taste and no longer keep going into the erroneous belief that there's something going on there and that there's an *I* who is responsible. So, when that belief is seen through, you can never actually believe it again. Even if the habit pattern comes up and you get trapped in the belief for a little while, in the recognition again and again, that belief will eventually fade away altogether. We don't have to work on this thought or that thought because the very working on them is an attempt by some entity to perfect itself. And that's an impossibility, because what you are is already the perfection itself, one without a second, the pure intelligence energy.

The reference point is the cause of all my problems. It's only a *me* that can be fearful. It's only *me* that can be full of self-pity, anger, resentment, unhappiness.

So *me* is the cause of the resentment, the anger, the fear, and all these things are the effects of that. And that's all that so-called karma is – cause and effect. What happens when I see the cause – this believed-in entity – is a fiction with no substance or independent nature? If I ask myself the simple question, "Can there be an effect without a cause?" I would then answer, "No, there can't possibly be an effect without a cause."

So if I'm not relating things to this imagined cause or entity, then the effects must drop away of themselves. And that's the way we can be rid of all this psychological suffering. Have a look. There's no entity in this body and if somebody calls me a nasty name, where's it going to lodge if I haven't related it to a reference point, an image? If it's got nowhere to lodge, where must it go? It must dissipate back into the emptiness from which it came because it is not taken delivery of.

Nisargadatta says, "Don't take delivery." He explains, "If the postman knocks on your door with a parcel containing a bomb and you don't take delivery of it, is it going to hurt you?" It's simply going to move on. If we don't take delivery of these things, it's just no big deal.

## Reflections on Nisargadatta

**Q:** *Was there a particular pointer from Nisargadatta that you found helpful?*

**Bob:** Well I can't say there was. There were probably many, and probably a lot of notions and ideas he said that would come up. But I can't say there was anything in particular. Just the fact that in seeing that something is false, you can't truly believe it again. You may get caught in it again – that's what seemingly happens because of old habit patterns – some discipline would come up through the mind, like, don't go there, or full stop, or wait a minute, who's this happening to – something like that. But it wasn't *me* thinking it – it couldn't be a *me* thinking it anymore. So where would it be coming from? It must be coming from the pure intelligence itself. If it's not attributed to an entity, it's just the same as the breathing and the living.

And the emotions come up too, you know. It's useless saying, "I'll never get angry again." (*Laughing*) Bang. You're into it before you know it. Why? It's the same as when I was a kid, I'd say that I'd never be a drunk. And if I saw a drunk, I'd say, "Fancy being like that. It'd never happen to me." But it did. Why? All points to prove that *I*, as the entity, never had any say in anything at all.

At one stage, the chatter would go on continuously all day. And it'd build up and up and up, until there would be all sorts of emotions and stresses in the body. But the whole lot can be dropped like that. It loses its hold because there is nowhere for it to lodge. As Nisargadatta says, "Nothing can trouble you except in your imagination."

**Q:** *I find the speaking opens up automatically to the most surprising people. The ones who I think would actually really be interested often can't hear anything past their own mind net.*

**Bob:** When I came back from Nisargadatta's I went back to the Fellowship, back to AA, as there were a lot of people who had helped me during those early years. Initially I tried to talk to some of them but they didn't want to hear it. I watched some of them die some very miserable deaths still locked up in the head and all their psychological suffering. So you learn. You don't have to cast it out there to everybody. Those who want to hear will come and find their way to you somehow or other, just as they did to Nisargadatta.

It never ceased to amaze me. You know, thousands of people would go past his door each day and you know what India is like. They didn't have a clue he was there, or who he was, or what he was. But just by sitting in that little slum room, people would come to him from all over the world. His book was out at that time, but there weren't many takers for that either. A few people would get it apparently and others would hear about it some way or other. People hear about these things in all sorts of amazing ways. Just like some of the people who come here. So it's amazing, someone gets onto them and drags them along.

**Q:** *So Bob, this understanding, this awakening that happened over 30 years ago. You mentioned the other day that over time your articulation of it has developed. What can you say about how it is just day to day?*

**Bob:** Nothing much to say about it. Sun comes up, moves around the sky then it goes down. Things happen and there's not much concern with any of it. If anything needs to get done it gets done or it doesn't. If it doesn't get done now it gets done the next day. There's not a wanting of anything much either. At the moment there are no particular desires whatsoever. Those moments when you might want something may come up. They are either fulfilled or not but it doesn't hang around and there's no carry-on like it once used to be.

**Q:** *When you look back in your life there was a particular personality, particular pattern, whether it was impatient, fiery and quick to anger or whatever. Do you see that basic personality pattern still there?*

**Bob:** That's what I call the natural characteristics that expresses through this pattern. Because the concepts are not taken on board here and the reference point or self-centre is not taken for the real, then there is no suffering.

**Q:** *So nothing has happened, nothing has changed?*

**Bob:** No, nothing has changed. The living is not from the point of a separate entity any more. You're just the livingness, the functioning, the patterning. You can't possibly go back and believe there is any entity there with any substance or independent nature.

If it's not there now then it could never have been there. Even though there was the quickness to anger and all the emotions came up, there was no entity doing that, though at the time it was believed that there was. It's just what is happening.

**Q:** *So what I'm hearing is that while it's the same, the difference is that it's not fed. So if something comes up, it flares up and then it dies down and is not fed and re-perpetuated. The difference is while it's the same, it's not attributed and the suffering isn't there.*

**Bob:** Yes. It's not some state or big deal, it's what's natural and it's not even thought about.

**Q:** *You just do whatever comes up?*

**Bob:** Whatever you are moved to do. Just like if a sickness comes upon you, you do whatever comes up in response to it. It might come through someone else that you are pointed to do this or that.

**Q:** *What happened when you went to see Nisargadatta?*

**Bob:** I just understood what Nisargadatta was pointing to.

**Q:** *What did he say that really got through to you?*

**Bob:** He said the only way he could help anyone was to take them beyond the need for further help. Well that's really implying it's the end of the search, isn't it? He did that by pointing out that I wasn't what I believed myself to be. I wasn't the body or the mind. And I could see that I wasn't the body; I wasn't the mind. What he was saying and pointing out continually was that it was all conceptual and all images and ideas, imaginings that I had about myself were not the truth.

**Q:** *What happened when you saw that?*

**Bob:** Well, it was a great sense of relief for a start and I said that I would never get caught in the mind again. Naturally, as soon as I stepped out of Nisargadatta's doorway, I got caught in the mind. Yet something had happened and I had seen through it. Even though the old habitual patterns started again, if you've seen the falseness of it, you can't actually believe anything anymore because it loses its intensity. All the imaginings, concepts and ideas that went on lost their intensity to a certain extent. And the more it was seen, then the less it seemed to matter. The seeing was immediate, and in the seeing I got that what he was saying was true. It was immediate, that there was nothing there really.

Just like the story of the fellow in the dark of night who steps on what he thinks is a snake. When he shines a torch on it and finds it is just a piece of rope, the sense of relief is immediate. However, the body's instinctual response of fear and trembling which was triggered by the belief that the rope was a snake, that takes a lot longer to die down. And that was the same here. Though there was an immediate seeing through it, the chatter would go on again. Poor me, blah, blah, blah… the resentment and the taking delivery of the things that were going on.

But you see, it wouldn't last because there was a remembering – "Hey, wait a minute, there's nothing there." So you break out of it, snap out of it again, and then go back into it again, and snap out of it again.

**Q:** *I heard that you had shouting matches with Nisargadatta, that you'd get up the front and you'd be yelling at him. What was that about?*

**Bob:** He was taking away all my concepts and the dearly held beliefs that I might have had as well as any ideas of things that I thought I'd understood. He'd kick everything out from underneath. He would never agree to anything anyone ever said to him, although he'd have a clear look at what someone was saying. As far as he was concerned, it was all conceptual. And even though there was a seeing of the most profound truth, that wasn't good enough either. So you were left with nowhere to stand. I might have some answers to the question and he'd knock them out. I'd fire up and argue about that a bit, yet I was continually left with nothing.

**Q:** *In that phase of understanding what Nisargadatta was talking about – understanding the truth, with the moving back to the old habitual patterns and catching it, and then seeing it again for what it is, do you think living in the ashram gave you basically some time out for it to all settle down?*

**Bob:** No. Before going to Nisargadatta's, I used to do all the ashram discipline very earnestly and sincerely. It had meant everything to me, but it all dropped away immediately.

**Q:** *So living in an ashram was probably no different than living anywhere else?*

**Bob:** No. As they say, "Cutting wood, carrying water." And even if I'd never gone back to Nisargadatta, it would have kept eating away and doing what it did anyway. Once you see something is false, you can never truly believe it again. And if you can't believe it, how can you keep going back into it? Little insights would come up and it got clearer in these discussions and arguments that Nisargadatta and I used to have. He used to sit me out at the front and get right into me. That was all very helpful of course, but probably wouldn't have been necessary. He was making sure there was nothing left, I guess.

**Q:** *You keep the teaching simple with nothing extraneous added.*

**Bob:** Yes, yes. And basically that's what has being spouted down through the ages; it's non-dual and there's only one. In all the religions there is only the one. It doesn't need to be divided up or complicated, does it?

Start from the fact that it's already *That* and stay with it. No matter what appears and what doesn't appear on it, it's still the one. Whether you call it consciousness, awareness, super-consciousness or whatever else – it's only conceptual. You can run *neti neti neti,* but you can also run the opposite which is "That's *That,* that's *That,* that's *That,*" because it is all *That.*

What has been bound or needs to be liberated? There was never anything that was ever bound, though it may seemingly have appeared to be. Who would want liberation in seeing that liberation was just a phantom anyway? You can't liberate a phantom.

**Q:** *Nisargadatta speaks about tenacity and a one-pointedness which takes you to the goal. Doesn't this imply time?*

**Bob:** He spoke to different people from all walks of life and someone who mightn't have the least clue about this may find a need to be tenacious or earnest at that stage. In that respect, you know, he was compassionate. Yet if he thought somebody was mucking around, he'd throw them out and get rid of them and wouldn't bother with them. Others, he would encourage.

**Q:** *Yes, like with Mark, he gave him a mantra because that's what he needed.*

**Bob:** Well, a lot of people would go and ask for a mantra and want him as their guru, especially the lot that were coming from the other ashrams. Nisargadatta would do the bhajans for morning and night – mainly for the Indian people to attend. He'd be out there chanting with the best of them, you know. The room would be thick with incense and they'd be banging their cymbals together and God knows what.

## Can You Get Out of the Now?

Most people worship the messenger, and in worshipping the messenger they miss the message. What we're pointing to here is the message. And I say I'm not speaking to anybody, I'm not speaking to any mind, I'm speaking to that *I am,* that I am – that sense of presence that expresses through the mind as the thought, *I am*. I'm not speaking to the thought, *I am*. I'm speaking to that which recognises and knows the *I am*. Just to this and nothing else.

In Hinduism they call it *Advaita* – meaning non-duality – and they try and describe it by saying it's *one without a second*. Even the idea of one implies that there could be other than one – so again bringing it down to its bare essence, there is only *That*. And that is the *Mahavakya,* or the great word, or the great mantra they use. I am *That*. Thou art *That*. This is *That*. That's *That*. All is *That*. And the *That* they are talking about is that sense of presence or essence.

The concepts I'm using are not it either. I can only use the term *That* because it can't be grasped by a concept – a concept is all mind stuff and you can never grasp it in the mind. If you stop imagining and anticipating, and stop recalling the past, where are you? You are in that immediacy which you've never left. So we've never actually moved away from this presence.

And all this crap about trying to live in the now, look at it the other way. Try and get out of the now if you can. Can anyone get out of the now? What's the point of trying to live in something you can't get out of? That's one of the traps we fall into. These things need to be looked at and seen because nobody's going to give you anything. You're not going to get anything.

Question some of the beliefs we've hung onto all our lives and you realise that the false cannot stand up to the investigation. Something that is not the truth will fall away and will be seen through and recognised as false. Once you see something is false, you can never actually believe it again. And a belief is never the actual. The dictionary definition of belief is *an unquestioned acceptance of something in the absence of reason; acceptance of an alleged fact, without positive knowledge or proof.* How many beliefs have you taken on board that you haven't got any positive knowledge or proof about?

Nisargadatta tells you clearly in one statement: "There's nothing that can trouble you except in your own imagination." When you investigate, you'll see that anything that troubles you is in your imagination, in the *imagining.* That word, *imagine* – image-ing – creating mental images or concepts. An image is not the real.

So what you're seeking you already are. Start from that fact and that makes the problem a lot easier. See you're already That and see through some of those false beliefs, and then there's nothing to look for. Then you've fallen right into what you've never left, what you've always been.

## Everything Appears in That Emptiness

**Q:** *People flock to see certain masters and have darshan with them. Isn't this "enlightenment" that is spoken about rather special?*

**Bob:** What could be so special about your natural state?

**Q:** *Sometimes people talk about having a taste of that singularity, the non-conceptual awareness. It seems to be short-lived and they hanker after it again. Why does it seem to go away?*

**Bob:** Well then again, the focus is on the taste. The taste is there in the immediacy and it seemingly moves on like everything. It is transient. They remember the taste and that becomes the reference point. They want to have the same taste and not leave it as a fresh and new expression. It might be what you call *a different taste*. But you understand it's coming from the same source. It is the pure *experiencing* in which experiences take place. Experiences come and go just as that taste came and went. What it appears on does not come or go.

**Q:** *So in seeing through this notion of* me, *what happens to the identity? How does functioning continue?*

**Bob:** Well it continues the way it always did. When it's not related to a *me* any more, in seeing through the *me*, what is it? It's just what's happening. It's the livingness itself, the life expressing. That is what you are... not the entity. We try to encapsulate that in this pattern of skin and bones. The pattern is appearing in that life and expressing through that pattern as life. There is only life, ever expressing.

**Q:** *Buddha said, "It is the mind that creates the world." Prior to that sense of am-ness, that sense of presence, there is no world as such.*

**Bob**: He says that it is the mind that creates the world, but what creates the mind? What does the mind appear in? It appears in that emptiness as an expression, a pattern appearing through that emptiness. Emptiness is form, forming as mind. From that form, the world, the universe, everything forms. Is anything ever other than the emptiness?

**Q:** *In the Dzogchen it says, "Whatever appears, let it rest in its uncontrived singularity." So everything is conceptual, even the singularity?*

**Bob:** There is still the idea or concept of one. And although it's appearing as other, it is still only *That*.

## There Is Nothing Wrong With Thought

**Q:** *Don't you need these concepts to exist in society?*

**Bob:** Yes. There's nothing wrong with a concept if you understand it as a concept. The problem is when the concept is believed to have some substance and some independent nature of itself. There is nothing wrong with thinking, nothing wrong with the mind. If it's understood, you see through it. But the belief in the mind makes it seemingly use us, instead of that essence that you are using the mind as a useful instrument. When it's believed to be what I am, it's self-destructive.

This building was an idea in someone's mind, so is the art on the wall, so is the technology – all an idea that's come through somebody's mind. That essence is expressing it through the mind. But at the other end of the scale, when it is believed to be me, it tells me I'm not good enough, or I'm fearful, or I'm only human, or I'm limited. So it's self-destructive when the mind is believed to be what I am. It produces all these limiting, negative ideas and concepts.

**Q:** *Don't people need to have these negative thoughts to work through?*

**Bob:** Well working through them is just like peeling the skin off an onion. You take one layer off and then go back and back again. I've seen people doing that for 20 or 30 years and they have never got anywhere. It might dawn on them that maybe they are looking in the wrong direction. What happens if you see that what you are working on is a fiction? You see that there's actually nothing there.

Ask yourself this question: *what is wrong with right now if I don't think about it?* To do that, you have to pause a thought. Now in dropping the thought, there is just pure wakefulness, awareness, being-ness. You can't say it's good, you can't say it's bad, you can't say anything. There is nothing wrong with right now unless I think about it. It's the thought that is the problem.

**Q:** *It makes sense that the entity is a fiction – however, the beliefs continue. Is there something that holds the beliefs in place and makes them continue?*

**Bob:** Ask yourself who has the belief, and the obvious answer is *me. I have the belief.* But what are you going to attribute the belief to if you haven't got that concept *me?* Bankei makes the statement that *everything is perfectly resolved in the unborn Buddha mind*. Everything is naturally resolving constantly and effortlessly. From a limited viewpoint, reference point, or self-centre, everything can seem chaotic and disorderly. But how substantial is the reference point if it's an appearance like everything else? It's an appearance we call *me*, or *I*, but it is not substantial. When there is a knowing and understanding of that, then there is a natural relaxation.

And in that recognition there is also a seeing or knowing that none of the appearance can ever last. It's constantly transient, constantly changing. The definition of reality is *That which never changes*. That emptiness which is not a vacuum or a void – a *cognising emptiness* – is the activity of knowing. Can you add anything to it? Can you take anything away from it? That knowing that you are is there in the immediacy, isn't it? You know that you are. That emptiness is suffused with an innate knowing or intelligence and not confined to one particular pattern, shape or form.

## There Is No Death

There is a story about a servant of a rich merchant in ancient Baghdad. The servant is walking down to the marketplace to get some vegetables for the master, and when he gets there he comes face to face with Death. Death looks at the servant with an astonished look on his face and frightens the hell out of him.

The poor servant runs back to his master and says, "Master, quick, quick, I've just come face to face with Death in the marketplace, and I fear he's going to take me. Lend me your fastest horse so I can flee to Samarra and so escape him." So the master agrees and the servant saddles up the horse, hops on it and flogs it out of the yard and across the countryside towards Samarra.

A couple of hours later the master goes for a stroll and he too meets up with Death. He says, "Hey, listen here, Death, what's the idea of scaring my servant the way you did?" And Death says, "I'm sorry. I didn't mean to scare him. It's just that I got such a surprise at seeing him here in Baghdad, when tonight I've an appointment with him in Samarra." So that's it. It's all story.

**Q:** *If everything is, then what is death?*

**Bob:** You're taking the idea of death from the point of view of the person, that a person has this life. We don't live a life, life is living you. Can you tell me when you were born?

**Q:** *No, I can't actually remember.*

**Bob**: Alright then. Can you tell me when you'll die?

**Q:** *No, I can't tell.*

**Bob**: So you've been imagining it, a time when you'll die. You can't tell me when you were born. If you have a look at it more closely, you'll see that life continually lives on life. Where can death be in that? Life comes out of life. Integration is happening right now. Cells are being replaced. It's all integrating. In so-called death, that all turns around. It moves in the opposite direction. Disintegration starts. In that disintegration, millions of enzymes start forming in a corpse and start devouring it and breaking it down.

Now they're life forms that are just as important and of equal value. In breaking down that body they're getting life from it. The worms and maggots and whatever else will get life out of it also. So life is living on life. The residual left might go into the earth and out of that a seed may get nourishment and sprout. That in turn grows and then something will eat its seeds, and something else will eat the thing that ate the seeds. So life is continually renewing and regenerating constantly in different patterns, different shapes and forms.

We've taken this pattern that we imagine we are as

so important. If you go out into the universe and look back to the earth, then where would you be? You'd be smaller than the microbes crawling on the skin. (*Rubs his arm*)

There's a tree out there with hundreds of pinecones on it and in each pinecone there are many seeds. Now they're not all going to germinate and sprout into trees, but the potential is there for that to happen. You see, life continually lives on life. Nature is prolific in its regeneration. That pure intelligence is not confined; it's suffusing every cell of every pattern. There is no separate entity that was born or could die.

The idea of birth came about when you started to learn to reason. That which was born is the self-centre. You'll see in some of the ancient texts, such as the prayer of St Francis, "It is only by dying that I can have eternal life." He's not talking about physical death. He's talking about dying to that self-centre, getting that out of the road. St. Paul tells us the same thing. He says, "I die daily." Again, he's not talking about physically dying. In dying to that self-centre, there is eternal life. When you take that entity out, what are you? You are life itself, which has no beginning and has no ending.

**Q:** *So Bob, when I die, my sense of self will disappear as my brain functioning stops. Is it possible for that total cessation of the sense of self to disappear while I'm alive?*

**Bob:** Yes, yes, if you know that there is no self there with any substance or any independent nature.

**Q:** *We're going to know that when we die?*

**Bob:** No, you can investigate and see that now.

**Q:** *It's a concept for me now, because I'm well and truly alive with a sense of self and an attachment to the feelings.*

**Bob:** Investigate that concept and see if there's anything there with any substance or independent nature, or is it just the pure seeing, hearing, tasting, touching, smelling, and actual functioning going on? The actual living-ness is just happening. You see, the body is integrating right now. It's replacing cells and so forth. Then the opposite comes about. Disintegration starts and it begins to fall apart. When that happens, millions of enzymes form and start to devour it. So that in turn is giving life to myriads of enzymes, and the worms and maggots and whatever else. In the end, there might be a bit of ash or residue which goes into the earth and that'll be food for something else.

So life is constantly living on life. There is no death whatsoever. Patterns form, patterns play around, patterns disappear, but of the essence itself, nothing can be added and nothing taken away. And that is what you are.

**Q:** *The thing that is most challenging at this particular point is accepting that the doing is happening, and relaxing into that. I feel I should be doing something.*

**Bob:** If you see that there's no personal doer-ship, then there can be no doer there. When you say, *I* should be doing, who are you referring to?

**Q:** *I hear what you're saying and it sounds like it's the truth, but it's difficult being able to integrate it into my life because of all the conditioning.*

**Bob:** Well then again, what conditioning is there if you don't think about it? What is there when you pause a thought?

**Q:** *Well, there's no conditioning really.*

**Bob:** There is none. So there is no need to be still working on your conditioning, believing it and carrying on. You've just seen clearly that there is no conditioning without a thought, so again, conditioning is all conceptual. And when it comes up, do you take delivery of it and say that *my conditioning* is making me see this or do that? You'll say that this is just another concept, it's not what I am so full stop. In that full stop, the presence of awareness is there in all its nakedness, unadorned by any concept.

So this is the actual, this moment. I can never live this moment again. If I'm not totally with the five senses wide open with un-fixated awareness, then I'm not really living. None of us are. Totally live with what is going on right now.

## Even One Is a Concept

Non-duality – one without a second. We say *without a second,* because even the idea of *one* implies that there could be other than one. So when we say *without a second,* it cancels that concept or belief that there could be anything other than one. Even that *one* is a concept to try and explain omnipotence, omnipresence, omniscience; total presence, total power, total intelligence.

Now most of you have been on what's called a spiritual search, and that search is always attempting to become one – to unite with God, or become one with God, or one with the essence. There aren't two to begin with, so this so-called search is an impossibility. It's simply impossible to become one when there's not even one. There is only that. Not two. There were never two.

So who is searching, and for what? One without a second is the totality already. It's there in all the great traditions; I am *That,* thou art *That.* They are all telling you that you already are *That.* And they sometimes call it *presence awareness,* or *emptiness, knowing* – there are many different labels. The struggle to become something, to become realised, to become enlightened, become one, is constantly keeping you out of presence.

Becoming implies a future time. It's conceptual; it's in the mind, out of presence. What we call presence is a concept of time also, but we use that to try and express the immediacy of this moment. What is the actuality with you right now? Isn't there an awareness of presence right where you are? I don't mean presence as being in any particular spot, but just the knowing that you *are*. In that singularity, that non-dual, one without a second, there cannot be a subject or an object, because that's the division again.

Now that awareness, the presence awareness that I'm talking about, can you divide that? It's not two things. Can you divide awareness from this presence, or presence from this awareness? Even though we're calling it two things, it can't be divided. If there's no subject or no object, there can be no so-called birth or death. Birth implies two things – a time and a place.

If time is just a concept, and a place means some point to start from, what point can be found in space? And without a point to refer to, can there be such a thing as time? Time has to have a beginning. Where does this presence awareness start from if it's not measured from any point? If the time and place are seen for what they are, just concepts, ideas and images in the mind, then when were you not? There is no place where you are not.

All our problems arise from the belief that "I am". So what is *I am*? Aren't they acquired words we've learnt? What are you without the words? When you're not translating that sense of presence into the thought, "I am", is that the end of you? And if there's such a thing as *I am*, then there must be *you are*. *I* and *you*. *I* and *not I*. *Me* and *other than me*. It's the belief that there's more than one. *Me* and something other. And that dualistic concept is what the search is all about. We've heard that God is one, so we're searching to become united with that one. The *we* I'm talking about is just a conceptual image we've got about ourselves. There never were two. In seeing that, realising that, wouldn't a lot of our problems dissolve with no reference point to fixate on? With the cancelling out of these so-called *opposites*... there is equilibrium. There is no separation, no division, and definitely no-one to have the problem.

## All There Is, Is Experiencing

**Q:** *How do you feel and function as an individual in the world?*

**Bob:** It is the experience-ing without creating an experienc-er and the experience. If I say "I experience this", it creates a pseudo-subject, an entity, an individual who's *experienced* something. But there couldn't be an experienc-er without that experience-ing. The ING on the end of it means there's something that's happening in the immediacy of the moment. The see-ing, the hear-ing, the taste-ing, the touch-ing, the smell-ing. The seeing before a see-er and a seen are created.

You see that they're not separate things – they're just two ends of the one stick. And there couldn't be an experienc-er without experiencing, couldn't be the experience without experiencing, couldn't be a see-er without see-ing, couldn't be the seen without see-ing. So you see the observer and the observed, the experiencer and the experience – are all conceptual. All they are is the experiencing. That's the actual functioning of what's going on. And if I haven't created a see-er, that seeing is still going on just as naturally as it did before. And the hearing, it's happening the same way as it always has. I cannot attribute it to any entity because I cannot find an entity here with any substance or any independent nature.

So I am empty of a reference point, a centre, but if that seeing and hearing is still going on and I can't find a centre to see from, it must be the emptiness itself where that cognising is happening from. Emptiness suffused with knowing, intelligence.

## You Are the Stillness

**Q:** *Do you sometimes feel sadness, but the difference is there is no fixation?*

**Bob:** The difference is when it's *my* sadness, or *my* fear, or *my* unhappiness, then it's a problem. If sadness, fear, unhappiness or disturbance, or whatever is not labelled, then it's free to flow, it's not being fixated on.

**Q:** *When you are in utter stillness, there's no conflict, there's no anything. How do I get there more often?*

**Bob:** You will never be in that stillness. You are the stillness. The stillness is expressing and what you call *you* is appearing in that stillness. So that's what you are. That's what you really are. That is the stillness. So what do you have to do to be still? There's more stillness in this room than there is movement. There's a little bit of movement here and there, but is that stillness contaminated or hurt by the movement? Go outside into the vastness of space. There is more stillness out there than movement. In the vastness of space the stillness overwhelms it. So what do you have to do to find stillness?

**Q:** *Be still?*

**Bob:** Just recognise that whether there's chatter or movement, or anything going on, it is going on in the stillness, because there couldn't be movement without stillness. Stillness is not something that has to be looked for.

**Q:** *Is non-duality the emptiness?*

**Bob:** It's cognising-emptiness. Emptiness suffused with knowingness. Look out there in nature and you see that the entire manifestation, which is all appearance, is suffused with that innate intelligence – the shape of a tree, the insect, the bird, the human forms, the galaxies, the patterns – it all implies that it's suffused with an intelligence, a livingness or a vitality. Some of us might be Hindu, Muslim, Buddhist, Christian, atheist, agnostic, or whatever, and if we use the term, *God* – we refer it to that concept we have about God and get confused. I use the term *intelligence energy*, but even the term *intelligence energy* is not it.

What I'm talking about in *intelligence energy* is the activity of knowing. There's nobody sitting here who is not knowing right now. And I don't mean the know-er and the known, but the activity of knowing. Nobody can negate a knowing that they are right now. And because knowing is happening in the immediacy of this moment, it's an activity and any activity is a movement of energy. So intelligence energy is the activity of knowing. And that's what each and every appearance is here right now. That activity of knowing is happening. That is what you are and that's nothing that can be grasped with a concept or a thought. It's ineffable, it's inexpressible.

This is the actuality of this moment. The only living that can ever happen is right in this moment. You can't live a moment ago. You can recall a moment ago. When you're recalling it, you're recalling it in the now, in the immediacy of this moment. That's the only life it's got. And you can't live a moment in the future. You can imagine and anticipate the future, but the actuality is right now. You haven't left this moment. Plans will be made, but it won't be *you* doing it.

What can be done in this moment is done, and then it's let go of. Seeming choices will be made, but there's no choice maker. Life goes on the way it will always go on. The idea of an entity is the cause of all your problems. Because when something comes up, we refer it to the *me* of past memory and lose spontaneity. Learn to rely on that spontaneous intuitive function. It knows better than what you and I do.

We've put limitations on it and we put up boundaries. We've built a cage of words and the word is never the thing. And then we put terms on it like, liberation, freedom, enlightenment and all these so-called spiritual connotations, and it becomes a task or a job. Instead of being, we are trying to become. And while there's that concept of becoming, we've seemingly moved away from omnipresence and we're in the trap again.

We may think that we have to do something and then we might become that. If I search and study and undertake spiritual disciplines then I will *become.*

When do you think that becoming is ever going to happen? Is there anyone sitting here who is not being now? Separate the being-ness if you can. Can there be anything simpler than that? Get a taste of your true nature and true essence, that birth-less, death-less, time-less, space-less, body-less, mind-less – pure functioning intelligence energy. No division, no separation whatsoever.

There was a bloke who came here from overseas and he said, "I've heard this all before. I didn't get anything. They were the same old pointers." You hear the pointers everywhere but you don't realise the potency of the pointers unless you take them on board. Muktananda used to tell a story and people didn't get what he was talking about either. The story was about the fellow who went to the guru and asked to be taught truth. The guru said, "Thou art *That*." The fellow thought, "Oh yeah, I've heard that a million times." So he went to another guru down the road.

This guru had a big flash ashram and plenty of followers and the fellow asked to be taught the truth. The guru told him he'd have to serve in the ashram for 12 years and then the guru would teach him the truth. The fellow agreed and the ashram manager organised some work for him. The only job available was picking up cow shit, so the bloke picked up cow shit for 12 long years. After the time was up, the fellow went to the guru and said, "I've served you faithfully for 12 years, can you please teach me the truth?" The guru looked at him and said, "Thou art *That*," and this time the fellow saw clearly what was being pointed to.

You know, the pointers are all here and they are the same old pointers, there is nothing new. But if you really take them on board, they'll shift you all right.

## There Was Never an Entity

**Q:** *You understand the* Kundalini *tradition. Can you speak about that please?*

**Bob:** When we look into *Kundalini,* it's non-duality anyway. Shiva is the static aspect and Shakti is the dynamic aspect. So it's intelligence energy again. Shakti is the female aspect and when she dances the world appears. In other words, the vibration starts and the world appears. So it's the same as what we say in non-duality. It's pure intelligence energy, patterning, shaping and forming. We've got this name *Kundalini,* but it's still the same essence that's doing the work anyway – there's no entity there at all, yet that is rarely taught.

Even the so-called transmission of Shakti – the transmission of energy, they might think that it comes from a guru, but it's just a natural movement of energy. It's the one energy expressing, shaping and forming as everything. There's nothing wrong with any of it if you look into it properly, but mostly there is the idea of an entity doing something and having to get somewhere. It prolongs the idea of a journey and the belief in an entity trying to get somewhere. It implies time and that idea seemingly moves us away from omnipresence.

And while there is the idea of meditation and of doing this and that, there is the idea of an entity trying to do something. It's still dividing the one into two aspects – male and female, but the whole lot is all of it. There is no separation and there never was. It's just the one intelligence energy.

**Q:** *By persisting with the question, "Who is this* me*", does that enquiry eventually wear the notion down?*

**Bob:** It doesn't need to be worn down. It's not even there. How can you wear something down that's not there? In investigating and having a look at this *me* that we think we are, you'll see that it is just a thought, isn't it? We are constantly referring to this mental image that we have of ourselves. We think that we are so-and-so and that we are this, that and the other and belief goes into it.

But when you look, you see that it's just a thought and there's nothing there with any substance or any independent nature. The thought, or the word, or the concept can't be the thing. So what are we going to refer to if there is no *me*? See that there's absolutely nothing there. Everything goes on the same way as it did before, but it's not attributed to some entity that's going to fix it, cure it or suffer because of it. There's nowhere for it to attach.

**Q:** *So what you sometimes call the natural functioning, is that what might be referred to as enlightenment, illumination, awakening, or a self-realisation?*

**Bob:** Well I suppose you could call it realising that

there is nothing there. You could just say it's that. But as far as enlightenment is concerned – who and what could be enlightened? It's just like a simple dawning. Just as you might be in a hurry to get to work in the morning and you dash out and slam the door behind you. A hundred metres down the road, it suddenly dawns on you that you have forgotten your keys. And all the while you've known you've left them there, but you hadn't really known until you remembered.

Well, I went to Nisargadatta and saw that there was no entity there at all. He said, "You're not the body, nor are you the mind." I had heard that many times before, but when he pointed it out, I saw clearly.

Am I this *I* thought that's been seemingly constantly with me? And how constant is it? When you look at it closely, it's not. We don't think, *I am, I am, I am* all day, or anything about *I*. There are only certain times throughout the day it'll come up. But the knowing that you are is constant. Now what is that knowing? Is it coming from any particular place? People may say, "Oh, it's in my head," or "It's in my brain," but is it? What can the brain do without that knowingness, without that life essence? And what's the life essence? It's nothing that you can find anywhere yet you see it all around you. You see it in every leaf, every insect, every bird, every atom and every human. You see that life essence and the way it's functioning in nature and in the universe.

**Q:** *So you're talking about a dawning, an awakening or realising that what you are is the knowing?*

**Bob:** You then realise that it was always so. It was just seemingly obscured, just like the keys on the table weren't remembered until it suddenly hit you. It's the same – you realise that the knowing was always and ever there. You could call that a dawning if you like, but the term implies that something needs to happen to someone, yet there was never any entity at any time that ever did anything. It's just that it was not recognised.

That's why it's called ignorance – it's not that we're stupid or dull; it means we ignore our true nature and focus into what's appearing. And that's what constantly happens. Rather than sitting with the no-thing, we attempt to immediately fit it into some concept, idea, or some imagining. We like to get stuck into the mind stuff all the time. But see that there's nothing there and you'll see that there never was an entity there. Thoughts are just a mental construct and thought has no power. They're just happening and they are all of the same essence. They're the same intelligence energy, patterning, shaping and forming as everything.

**Q:** *So this understanding which totally denies the reality of any 'I' makes a joke of any concept of enlightenment.*

**Bob:** Yes, any idea of an entity, a person or individual takes you away from what the ancients clearly tell us. You'll see it in all the scriptures – omnipresence, omnipotence, omniscience – the base of all the teachings has been that. One without a second – non-duality. It doesn't leave room for anything at all that can be outside of it.

The appearance is still that reality, but not how it's appearing. It's appearing as this and that, just as this body appears to be a solid made up of elements, of air, earth, fire, water, space. Those elements can be broken down into sub-atomic particles, into nothing – *no-thing*-ness. But it's all energy, and what is energy? We can see how energy expresses and patterns, but we can't understand or grasp what energy is. And that can express and pattern in many different shapes and forms. You cannot see or grasp the wind, but you can see the way the wind expresses. It may move a flag, make the branch of a tree sway, or blow a bit of paper around. They are expressions of it. You can't see the wind itself, or know the wind.

**Q:** *Non-duality is often expressed as being one without a second. Is there a one?*

**Bob:** Well one implies that it could be other than one, but it's really *no-thing.* Now, can you say *no-thing* is one? There's *no-thing,* there's no manifestation, no pattern, but it's the un-manifest. What can you say about the un-manifest? Can you say that the un-manifest is one? It's *no-thing.* It can't be grasped with any concept whatsoever. It hasn't got a centre to it. It hasn't got a circumference or any dimension. And that's why they put *one without a second* on it because even the idea of one implies that there could be other than one. And no-thing... *no-thing* ever happened, yet it really is the source of everything. And the everything is nothing but the *no-thing* appearing as other. So in that way it encompasses everything and the nothing. It encompasses both the opposites.

**Q:** *Can you talk about space and time being the same thing?*

**Bob:** Well space is volume really, isn't it, and time is duration?

**Q:** *Yes.*

**Bob:** Now for me to get from here to where you are, does it take duration, take time? If it wasn't for the volume, would there be any need to get from here to there? So they're really one and the same thing. Again, it brings it back to the non-duality of everything. And you see that couldn't happen if there wasn't a *me* and a *you* first – there wasn't a centre for it to be measured from. That duration and the seeming apparent entity have to be in the volume. There can be no distance without measuring from some point.

**Q:** *So do reference points still keep coming up?*

**Bob:** Yes. Just the same as choices are seemingly made, opinions are seemingly held, and reference points seemingly come up. But knowing that there's nothing there for them to attach on to, they don't hang around. That's the difference. They're not fixated on and clung to. They are free to move on.

**Q:** *In a sense, though, the reference points seem to be useful to exist in this world.*

**Bob:** Yes, but there is no psychological trouble in any of that, is there? It's just a natural function of the living-ness. Things get done or don't get done, or whatever. Referring to this conceptual entity that we believe ourselves to be – that's where all the suffering comes from. That's all that can ever be seemingly hurt or touched.

But when you look in nature, can you see a reference point anywhere? Is there anything in nature where other things are being measured from? Does the earth in its orbit around the sun say, "I'm this far today and I'll be a bit closer to the sun at the end of next week". Do the comets in the outer reaches of the solar system say, "I'll soon be heading back towards earth"? The reference point measured from is from the earth and the earth's constantly moving too, so how can you say it's a valid reference point? In relation to space, where is the earth? Is it here or there or wherever?

## Everything Is That

So there is nothing other than *That*. You are that intelligence energy that's never been divided. That's why the sages down through time tell us that it's *one without a second*. There is only *That* – omnipresence, omnipotence, omniscience. Grasp what they're saying and you've got the answer right away. There is only *That*. They call it the *Mahavakya*, the great word. I am *That*, thou art *That*, this is *That*, that's *That*. Everything is *That*.

And what is the *That*? It is nothing that can be grasped by a concept. It is no-thing. It hasn't got any shape or form and it hasn't got any place where it can be latched onto or grasped. That's why they tell you in the Gita, the sword can't cut it, the fire can't burn it, the wind can't dry it, and the water can't drown it. It contains all of those things. They're all expressions of it. None of those things can contain it. Non-duality means exactly that – no room for dualism in it.

So the appearance is the one essence expressing and appearing as everything. Everything is still that one essence. It's never changed. In seeing the false as false, you don't have to find the truth, you're left with truth. So in that respect, there's nothing that an entity can do about it at all, because an entity has no power. And recognising is exactly what it is – re-cognising, because you already innately know it, it's already been cognised. You've tasted it and touched it, all your life. It's just a matter of re-cognising.

We put a label on awareness, the knowing that you are. Consciousness, awareness, being-ness, essence – we use many different concepts. If you pause that thought, there's an innate knowing that you *are*. It's not being translated by any concept. It has never had any beginning and has no ending. It is birthless, deathless, timeless, bodiless, mindless, beginning-less and endless.

That is what you actually are – not the thing. It's expressing, patterning, living, vibrating, forming and shaping, and it's every-thing. So the things are all patterns or appearances of that one essence. Our problem is that we've taken the appearance to be the reality. That's why in the scriptures they'll call it ignorance – it's not that we're dull or stupid, but we ignore our natural state. We ignore our true nature and focus into the appearance and try to alter, modify or correct the appearance.

There are many reflections appearing in that mirror over there. Trying to alter or modify things would be like one of those reflections trying to fix up another reflection. What hope has it got? What do you think might happen if there is the realisation that you are that essence and not the appearance you've taken yourself to be? What if it dawns on you that there is no reference point or self-centre with any substance, independent nature or reality whatsoever?

In just letting the natural functioning happen, you realise there's no one who is letting it happen. So just be. Just be what you actually are and see what happens from there. Realise that if there's no entity there now, then when were you? When could it ever have been real? If you see something is a fiction, it must have always been a fiction. So you must realise that all the living that has gone on in that so-called appearance has never been done by you, the entity. It grew you from the sperm and the ovum – there was no one saying that I must put a little finger on today, or a nose, or something like that, while you were growing. Never at any time have you done anything. So you've been lived all the way through. All the thoughts, feelings, emotions and expressions of that awareness that have happened through that pattern have never been done by you. So see that. Re-cognise what you already are.

## Staying with the Immediacy

**Q:** *It feels like thinking is clouding that pure awareness. I wish there were a reflex that would just pause a thought.*

**Bob:** It will happen by itself. For a start, it might not be quite so frequent because they're habit patterns and it's easy to fall back into them. So question and have a look because it can happen anywhere. You don't have to sit in meditation, although you can. You might be standing, walking, eating, doing whatever. That sense of presence is everywhere. It's what I call a natural meditation. There is no-one to meditate and nothing to meditate on. Recognise your own essence – the essence that you are. You can't find a centre anywhere, not in the mind, nor in the body. So what's seeing? Without a centre the seeing is still happening, appearing is still happening, thinking is still happening. If it's not coming from a centre, where's it coming from?

It is the emptiness itself that is suffused with knowing or intelligence. The thoughts are coming from that, and so too are the feelings and emotions and the energy that's patterning this body. It's all coming from the emptiness. The emptiness has got no dimension to it whatsoever. There is no centre or circumference.

***Participant:*** *And when you get that about yourself then the extension is that it's all immediately true for every* *other human being. So if somebody does something to you, it's not personal. There was no-one doing anything deliberately, something just happened and patterns interacted.*

**Q:** *So do you still get caught up in your thoughts?*

**Bob:** The thoughts will seemingly come and go and the discipline comes up of itself. There may be thinking and the thought *don't go there* or simply *full stop* might appear. Yet there's no entity thinking that thought or trying to do something about it. There will be activities that go on just the same as before. The difference is that it can't be applied to a *me*. That has all dropped off.

If you're not getting involved in the conceptualising, there's more chance of it arising naturally of itself. Because it's gone into the heart rather than the head, it will express in its own thoughts and words and they might be different to how they express here.

When we try to nut it out with our head, we get into the division again. That's why I say, "I'm not speaking to any body, I'm not speaking to any mind, I'm speaking to that *I am* that I am, to that sense of presence and knowing that you are – just this and nothing else." And it's not an entity speaking. It's that *I am*, that sense of presence speaking to that sense of presence. Where's the division? Where's the separation in that? You are *That*.

***Participant:*** *There's another important point and that* *is there's nothing to acquire. If you take the form of a seeker, then you're seeking something, and you want to get it. Go to the core of the belief system, which is the* me. *See through that. Have a look. Once that is seen through, all of the other beliefs collapse because they've all been referred to the* me *anyway.*

**Bob:** Just stay with the immediacy of what is now, instead of chasing. The mirror doesn't chase after the reflections. What we're doing is chasing after concepts in the mind. Be the mirror. You don't have to go anywhere; it's what's all appearing. You've never really moved away from it. Whatever seems to be chasing after them, is just another concept. A mirror doesn't move; there's nowhere to go.

**Q:** *So I'm not trying to stop my physical sensations?*

**Bob:** No. Those physical sensations are a natural functioning of the body. But the fear and anxiety are all thought-based and they don't need to be there. The so-called fear, anger, happiness and all the responses are just the natural functioning. When a sensation comes up which we might call anger, where are we naming that anger from? The past. If you're being with that sensation just as it is in the moment, is it anger if you haven't got a label for it? It's just what is.

As soon as we've thought, "Oh, this is anger and I shouldn't be angry", we've loaded it down with all the previous angers we've ever had, and it becomes overwhelming and takes over. Then the chatter goes on, we struggle with it, we build resistance and that resistance keeps it there. It doesn't give it a chance to dissipate because it's the mind resisting the mind. It hasn't got a chance to escape.

**Q:** *So Bob, do you meditate?*

**Bob**: Meditation implies there's somebody that's trying to meditate in order to get somewhere. True meditation is when you see there's no-one to meditate and nothing to meditate on. And that's the natural meditating – what they call *undistracted non-meditation,* where even trying to meditate would be a distraction.

**Q:** *Yes, you'd be trying to do something.*

**Bob:** However, you might simply sit down and just drop into meditation. But no deliberate doer is doing something and that's the important thing to see. It's that believed-in entity that's the cause of all your problems. Question that and see if you can find anything there. When you see for yourself that there is nothing there with any substance or any independent nature, all your problems lose their sting. There's no reference point to refer them to.

## There is No Separation

***Participant:*** *The two things Bob keeps on nailing are, there is no individual entity and there is no time. And I can only exist in time. Without time, there is no entity. So the whole thing of a journey to get a result simply recreates an entity locked in a double bind.*

**Bob:** And that's the only problem we've ever had – believing there is a seeker searching for something. That came about when the little child was about two years old, when he started to reason. Up until then, the little child is seeing everything just as it is. He's got no sense he's separate from anything. But the capacity of reasoning starts when he learns words from his parents. They tell him that he's a good little boy, he's this, that and the other – all sorts of concepts are put on him. So the little child learns words like *I* or *me*, and what's the opposite of *I* or *me*? *Not I*, or *not me*. So while he'd been seeing everything just as it is, now he's reasoning that's not *I*, or that's not *me*. The sense of separation develops when he sees something that's not *I*, or not *me*, and believes he's separate from it. And that's what separation is – an erroneous belief.

So with that sense of separation comes insecurity and vulnerability. If you feel separate from something, you feel isolated and there is insecurity and vulnerability. And when that starts, away we go.

The little child likes a warm and loving family around him. If he's got a loving family, he'll feel much more secure and less vulnerable. In the old days, families would form into tribes and feel more secure. Today we form into nations, and nations go to war for that very same reason – always frightened what the nation next door will do. They have more oil and threaten my security, so I'll invade them and take them over. And so it goes on.

The problem is we're looking out there – we try to become whole or complete by acquiring, amassing and accumulating. Our schools, our nations, our society teach us these things. We're always trying to become something – to become complete – not realising that we were never separate in the first place. *Becoming* implies time, a future time, and that is not omnipresence. The ancients have told us clearly that it's omnipresence, omnipotence, omniscience. Not three things, but three aspects of the one thing – total presence, total power, total intelligence. Total. And that doesn't leave room for a *you* or a *me*. There is no separation in omnipresence.

## The Actual Livingness Is Right Now

Well, can anybody actually live in the past? Can anybody actually live a moment ago? Try living a moment ago. Try living five minutes ago. Try living last week. You realise you can't. You can recall five minutes ago, you can recall last week or last year. The only actuality you're giving it is what you're giving it in this moment of recollection. You can't tell me what you did five minutes ago unless you recollect it and recall it. So you see you've got no hope of living in the past at all. The past is dead and gone. It's only now.

The same with the future: you can anticipate and imagine the future, but can you live in the future? You can't. What you are anticipating and imagining, you can only do it in the now, in the actuality of this moment. This is the actuality. It's always the actuality of this moment. The rest is fiction. What we add or what we take away might make it seem past and future, but the actual livingness is right now.

And see what happens if we're not actually living totally: we're living in the head as most of us do, in an imagined yesterday and tomorrow. We're missing out on a lot in life really, because while that total head stuff is going on, we're ignoring the seeing, the hearing, the tasting, touching and smelling. These other functions are going on in the body, and you vaguely know or hear something else in the background, or see something else in the background, but it's not the focus of attention. The main focus is in that thinking, and so we're not really living fully.

That's why they say in one of the Buddhist texts, "Be utterly awake with the five senses wide open. Be right with what is now with the five senses wide open; the hearing, seeing, tasting, touching, smelling, thinking – all equally." And it goes on to say, "Be utterly open with un-fixated awareness, where there is no fixating or clinging to some particular thought, idea or concept to the exclusion of the livingness." See what a difference that makes in living.

## The Taste of the Wakefulness

Is there anybody who is not awake right now? If you are not asleep, then you must be awake. And when you woke up this morning, first there was wakefulness and then everything appeared. From that moment on, everything appears in that wakefulness. All the events, experiences, thoughts, feelings and emotions – everything that is going on around you appears in that wakefulness. Have a look at it. Isn't the present wakefulness? It's not the wakefulness you had five minutes ago, nor the wakefulness that you might have in five minutes' time, it's the present one.

Without that wakefulness, would it be appearing? And what do you have to do to find wakefulness? Do you have to ask, "Am I awake?" Yet we do that, we try to grasp with a concept. All you have to do is realise that you are not asleep. If I'm not asleep, what must I be? There's no need to look for it. It's actually there. All that needs to happen is to leave it unaltered, unmodified, uncorrected. Get the taste of the wakefulness.

## Everything Appears on That Wakefulness

**Q:** *There's something in me that wants to eventually be awake more than being asleep, but right now I kind of go back and forth. There'll be moments of knowing, of clarity, and then I get lost. Can I be awake all the time?*

**Bob:** Have a look. You woke this morning, didn't you? You woke up, just the bare wakefulness. You opened your eyes, you were awake.

**Q:** *Yes.*

**Bob:** You got up, you got dressed, you breakfasted, and you've done this, that and the other. Thoughts and things have come and gone. And you've got here, you're sitting here. Now has that wakefulness changed, the wakefulness itself?

**Q:** *No.*

**Bob:** Things have appeared on it that didn't appear when you were asleep. While those things have appeared and disappeared, the wakefulness itself hasn't changed. Wakefulness hasn't been contaminated or touched by any of the things that have gone on mentally. You can't grasp or hold on to wakefulness in any way, shape or form with a concept. What could you add to that wakefulness, that ordinary wakefulness? What can possibly be added to it?

**Q:** *Nothing.*

**Bob:** What can be taken away from it?

**Q:** *Nothing.*

**Bob:** Can it get any deeper?

**Q:** *No.*

**Bob:** It's so obvious and simple that we miss it.

**Q:** *I keep thinking that it's some sort of state that I will be in, a state that will never change.*

**Bob:** Well, while that thinking about it is going on, you're trying to *become* instead of *being*. There's only being-ness. There's no becoming. Becoming implies a future time.

**Q:** *Does the full gamut of emotions display on this awareness? Do you get sadness or anxiety, or even excitement? Do all of those emotions display on that?*

**Bob:** Up until you started the investigation, you had believed that all those things were happening to an entity. Now that you've investigated, you see that there is absolutely no entity there with any substance or independent nature. And in seeing that, you must realise that there never was an entity. Did all the emotions and things appear before that happened?

**Q:** *Yes.*

**Bob:** Then who were they happening to?

**Q:** *They were just happening.*

**Bob:** Right. Well do you think they're going to stop now?

**Q:** *No.*

**Bob:** If the feelings and emotions are not being fixated on, then they're free to move on. They are just playing out in the moment so they don't hang around. It's just like the seasons coming and going. They're not in opposition with each other. We have this reference point, which is conceptual and made up of ideas, images and thoughts, past events and experiences. Experiences come and go but then we label them. A feeling arises and we refer it to this previous labelling, "Oh that's pain", or "That's anxiety." Without the labelling, thoughts and feelings just arise and subside. It's just as it is in nature. Nature is not worrying about whether it's cold and dark, or a wintry or hot day. It's not touched by the weather. So then, is the space-like awareness touched? It's daylight now. In a little while it'll be dark. Now, is space itself dark? Is it light?

**Q:** *Neither.*

**Bob:** And those things have appeared – darkness has come, yet light is latent in the darkness and darkness is latent in light. They appear and play around but the space is untouched. So everything – everything, appears in space. You are nothing but the content of space and appearance in space. Every thing, every object is transient. It comes and it goes. Even the elements can fall apart and disappear. But will space itself ever disappear?

## I Am That Presence Awareness

I am that *presence awareness,* that essence. I can't be anything else. I am eternity. Eternity cannot be measured. Eternity is now. Eternity is timeless because it has no beginning and no ending. Do you have any beginning or any ending? As a believed-in entity, you can imagine a point in time when you began, and you can imagine or anticipate a point in time when you will finish. The pattern breaks down and dissolves back into that essence. But what happens to that in which this pattern appears? Can you put a point of time on that anywhere?

What has been with you from as far back as you can remember? Isn't it that same knowingness that's with you right now – not the content, not knowing this or that, but the pure knowing itself which you cannot negate? Is that a vacuum or a void, or is there a vividness, a clarity of livingness? Does that have to be started up? Does it have to be stayed with and be constructed, or is it something that cannot be conceptualised or labelled?

We call it a thing, but it's not even a thing, because all things and every thing appear in it and are just expressions of it. And there is the capacity for it to express in all of its diversity. That's the wonderment, the miraculous-ness of it, if you like to use those terms. In the recognition, wouldn't you rejoice in *I am That,* and let it be?

The functioning is constantly happening and vibrating into opposites. In essence, a pattern is the one thing. Can you separate the heat from the flame? Can you separate the wetness from the water? Can you separate this apparent body, this pattern of energy, from the space, the air, the water or the fire, which is patterning, shaping and forming it? So that's all that's necessary to see. It is still that one without a second.

And it's still going to appear as a separate body, a separate entity. Things are still going to happen, still appear as the pairs of opposites. There'd be no manifestation without it. All sorts of activities can take place in a dream during deep sleep. You may dream you're in the city or in the country. You may dream you are on a mountain or out on the ocean and there may be other people in the dream.

Where are these activities taking place? What substantial thing is it taking place in? When you wake up from the dream, which is seemingly vivid and very real while you're in it, where has it gone? How substantial and how real was it?

So when we say there's nothing to acquire or get in the way of enlightenment or realisation, that's what we mean – there is nothing. You are simply already *That*. You are *That*.

## About the Author

Kalyani Lawry lives in Melbourne, Australia. She compiled and edited a series of Bob's CDs and co-produced his recent DVDs. Kalyani and her husband Peter hold weekly Nonduality groups and offer private consultations.

**For further information about this book and related websites, please visit:**

Peter and Kalyani Lawry's website:
www.nonduality.com.au

Non-Duality Press:
www.non-dualitypress.com

Sailor Bob Adamson's website:
http://members.iinet.net.au/~adamson7

## NON-DUALITY PRESS

If you enjoyed this book, you might be interested in these related titles published by Non-Duality Press.

*Oneness*, John Greven
*Awakening to the Natural State*, John Wheeler
*Shining in Plain View*, John Wheeler
*Right Here, Right Now*, John Wheeler
*You were Never Born*, John Wheeler
*The Light Behind Consciousness*, John Wheeler
*What's Wrong with Right Now?*, Sailor Bob Adamson
*Presence-Awareness*, Sailor Bob Adamson
*You Are No Thing*, Randall Friend
*The Wonder of Being*, Jeff Foster
*An Extraordinary Absence*, Jeff Foster
*Dismantling the Fantasy*, Darryl Bailey
*Standing as Awareness*, Greg Goode
*The Transparency of Things*, Rupert Spira
*Awakening to the Dream*, Leo Hartong
*From Self to Self*, Leo Hartong
*Already Awake*, Nathan Gill
*Being: the bottom line*, Nathan Gill
*Perfect Brilliant Stillness*, David Carse
*I Hope You Die Soon*, Richard Sylvester
*The Book of No One*, Richard Sylvester
*Awake in the Heartland*, Joan Tollifson
*Be Who You Are*, Jean Klein
*Who Am I?*, Jean Klein
*I Am*, Jean Klein
*The Book of Listening*, Jean Klein
*Eternity Now*, Francis Lucille

# MICH
# JORDEN

## AN INSPIRATIONAL BIOGRAPHY OF ONE OF BASKETBALL'S GREATEST PLAYERS

Kyle Robinson

# MICHAEL JORDEN

## AN INSPIRATIONAL BIOGRAPHY OF ONE OF BASKETBALL'S GREATEST PLAYER

Kyle Robinson

By Kyle Robinson

Cover Design : Kyle Robinson

Printed in the United States of America

**Table of Contents**

# Introduction

Some players from the city of Chicago, Illinois, became well-known in their respective sports. They've all achieved personal achievement and are Hall of Famers in their respective leagues and sports. During their playing careers, some of them even won a championship or two. Walter Payton of the National Football League's Bears, Ernie "Mr. Cub" Banks of Major League Baseball, and Bobby "Golden Jet" Hull of the Blackhawks are among these athletes.

During his 15 years with the Chicago Bulls in the National Basketball Association, however, no other athlete had ever earned as many awards as Michael Jordan. Jordan will always be remembered for wearing the red and black of Chicago, joining the list of aforementioned Chicago sports superstars, despite only playing two years of his career with the Washington Wizards.

A bronze sculpture of Jordan's signature "jumpman" position stands in front of the United Center, which many regard to be the house that Jordan built, over 20 years after his final season with the Bulls. Many people in Chicago will never forget his name because he was responsible for six titles in the 1990s. His classic number 23 uniform is still worn by many admirers. As the Bulls strive to reclaim their heyday from 20 years ago, current stars like Derrick Rose are held to the same standards.

There's a reason Jordan had one of the best NBA careers of all time, and one of the best professional sports careers of all time. Clothing, pop culture, film, music, and other sports, like as baseball, all bear his name. But it all started with his basketball achievements, which include more than 32,000 points, six Most Valuable Player trophies, and several individual honors for both offense and defense.

Basketball "has been everything," Jordan once declared. It's my safe haven, the location where I've always gone when I needed comfort and calm. It's been the location of excruciating anguish as well as exhilarating delight and happiness."

But his brilliance went well beyond individual championships and even NBA Finals trophies. Jordan was responsible for a number of unforgettable events that NBA fans still discuss today. Few players have 50-point games or play in a crucial championship game while suffering from a stomach virus, dubbed the "Flu Game."

The nicknames were numerous - Air Jordan for his dunking; His Airness for his airness; and Money for his ability to consistently score 20 or more points. He was also a sure-fire assurance of giving fans something unique every night.

In the 1990s, everyone wanted to "be like Mike" because of his scoring prowess, championship wins, and work ethic.

# Chapter 1: Childhood and Adolescence

Every legend begins with a humble beginning, and Michael Jeffrey Jordan's journey began on February 17, 1963, when he was born as the fourth of five children in Brooklyn, New York. Michael's parents, James and Delores, were concerned a few years after his birth as the nasty streets of Brooklyn lured them with drugs, booze, and violence. As a result, the family relocated to Wilmington, North Carolina, a much smaller, quieter town that some believe is better for raising a family.

This is the Jordan family's residence. While raising their family, his father, James, worked at an electric plant and his mother, Delores, worked at a bank. Michael has two older brothers, Larry and James, as well as a younger sister, Roslyn, and an older sister, Delores. His parents emphasized the importance of instilling in their children a desire to work hard and achieve their goals.

Michael used to play sports for pleasure when he was younger. However, he was sometimes discouraged by the fact that his older brother, Larry, consistently outperformed him. His father also believed that Larry, who was a year older than Michael, possessed the family's true basketball potential. Despite this, the two would play and make their own games in their massive backyard, which consisted of around five acres of property plus another 13 acres owned by family.

Michael's father believed Larry had the skill in part because Michael was not very tall when he was younger, and there was no indication that this would change since no one in the family had ever surpassed six feet.

James, his other brother, was succeeding in life, but not as an athlete. He enlisted in the US Army and served until 2006, when he retired as a command sergeant major. He was a member of the 35th Signal Brigade, which was part of the XVIII Airborne Corps.

Throughout his boyhood, Jordan continued to play football, baseball, and basketball. Surprisingly, his favorite sport at the time was not basketball. Baseball, on the other hand, was his favorite pastime. He was designated a top performer in his youth league for his pitching and outfield work when he was 12 years old. When he represented his team in a state competition, he was also chosen the most valuable player.

Michael was not a young, well-groomed lad at the time. In truth, he had been suspended for fighting at the age of 12 and had previously participated in numerous bouts in the halls. When he wasn't in school, his mother, Delores, wouldn't allow him sit at home and watch TV. She drove him to work with her and made him read in the car all day, just in front of the bank window. His mother took him to the library after work, where she had a friend who worked there, and made sure he read more.

Michael, a 15-year-old student at DC Virgo Junior High School, was an all-around athlete who participated in three sports. He was not, however, a zealot for any of them. As he entered high school at Emsley A. Laney High Institution, no one expected him to pursue a career in sports, but the school provided a rocky start for the young heir to NBA royalty.

## High School Years

In 1978, the start of his high school basketball career did not go as planned. During his sophomore season, he intended to fill the open roster position for the Buccaneers' playoff run. They went with his friend, LeRoy Smith, and it was a good decision. Jordan was only five feet ten inches tall, whereas his friend Harvest Leroy Smith stood about six feet and a half inches tall, a good height for high school basketball. Jordan, on the other hand, was only slightly over average in terms of shooting and bad in terms of defense. Coach Clifton Herring (commonly known as "Pop") would assign him to the junior varsity team. Smith was the lone sophomore at Emsley A. Laney High School in Wilmington, North Carolina, who was going to try out for the varsity team.

While many people are familiar with Jordan's fame, few are aware that Smith had some success in the sport as well. After beating out the soon-to-be NBA champion, the sophomore accepted a four-year sports scholarship to play basketball for the University of North Carolina in Charlotte — not the same team that wears the renowned "Tar Heel" blue and white. Rather, it was the Charlotte 49ers' green and gold, and he was allowed to be the senior captain who led all Sun Belt Conference teams in rebounding. Smith went on to play in the Premier English Basketball League, the German Basketball League, the United States Basketball League, and the Japan Basketball League in the mid-1980s and early 1990s. While he was a team leader in points, rebounds, and blocks, he never made it to the NBA and ended up in the business world, where he is now the vice president of sales and marketing for NBC Universal's TV Distribution chapter.

The loss of a varsity slot was the catalyst for things to turn around, as Jordan embraced the setback as incentive to better for next year and work harder on his basketball talents in the hopes of making the varsity team. Every day, he practiced with his brother Larry. Between his sophomore and junior years, he grew an extra five inches to 6' 3". His work ethic was clear as he was first in line for conditioning drills and ran as hard as anybody, which coaches notice, especially if it's a guy they didn't pick, and are pleased to see someone use it as inspiration rather than taking it negatively and not working as hard in practice.

Jordan improved dramatically during his sophomore season, and he was one of the reasons fans attended to the JV games, which were held a few hours before the varsity game. He had a couple games in which he scored more than 40 points. Jordan scored 45 points in the team's 71-58 triumph over East Carteret on

December 5, 1978, in the first of those contests. Jordan will score 44 points to help the squad upset Southern Wayne 88-67 on January 29, 1978, nearly two months later. Fans came out to see Jordan score a lot of points and become a star player even though he wasn't playing in the varsity main event game that night – whether he scored 24 points against East Carteret on December 15, 1978, or only six points against New Hanover on February 16, 1979 – fans wanted to see Jordan entertain them with his skills and hustle on every play.

Jordan never received a call-up during his sophomore year, despite his strong numbers and the attention he drew for the junior varsity team. After getting cut from the varsity team, it only encouraged Jordan to become more competitive. He acted as if he wanted to ensure that it never happened again.

Jordan averaged close to 25 points per game for a 4-A squad — North Carolina's highest classification during his junior season on the varsity team. Jordan scored 35 points in his debut varsity game, an 81-79 victory over Pender High School on November 30, 1979. Jordan would score 28 points in a loss against Southern Wayne on December 11, 1979, just a few games later. On December 18, 1979, he scored 31 points in a 69-57 victory over Kinston. Jordan then went on to score 29 and 30 points against New Bern (on December 21, 1979) and Wadesboro-Bowman (on December 21, 1980). (December 27, 1979).

He would later score 40 points in a 72-64 loss against Goldsboro on January 2, 1980, after hitting 17 total field goals. A few months later, on February 14, 1980, he set a season record with 42 points after making 18 field goals in a 73-60 win over Eastern Wayne. Jordan scored 20 points in the Laney Buccaneers' 73-60 triumph on February 18, 1980, and another 18 points in the team's 40-35 loss against Southern Wayne on February 20, 1980, just before Jordan helped the Laney Buccaneers to the North Carolina Division II playoffs. Jordan concluded the year with a total of 22 games played and an average of 24.8 points per game as the Buccaneers finished with a 14-10 varsity record. He'd keep improving, and he'd begun to gain a following among numerous college basketball programs in the area.

During the summer that followed, he wowed college scouts at Howard Garfinkel's Five-Star Basketball Camp, where he often played one-on-one with other top high school players. In his final year with the Buccaneers, he guided his high school to the top of the state rankings, finishing the season with a 19-4 record. They would go on to win their first five games, with Jordan scoring 33 points in the season opener against Pender in a 76-65 victory, and then scoring 27 points on 12 field goals in a road win against the same Pender team on December 5, 1980. Jordan scored 21 points in the Buccaneers' 57-46 win over Southern Wayne on December 9, 1980, and 28 points in the Buccaneers' 73-71 road victory over Hoggard on December 12, 1980.

Jordan reached the 30-point barrier six times during the season, with his best effort coming on February 3, 1981, when he scored 39 points in a 64-56 victory over Kinston after making 11 field goals and 17 of 19 free throws. Jordan would once again lead the Buccaneers to the state's Division II playoffs, which began with a 55-28 thrashing of Eastern Wayne on February 23, 1981. Jordan had 27 points in that game, only three days after scoring 26 points in a 70-38 triumph against the same squad to close the regular season. After a 56-52 loss against New Hanover in the conference title game on February 25, 1981, Jordan and his Laney teammates were unable to win the state championship, much as the previous season. Jordan scored 26 points in the game after hitting eight field goals and going 10 for 18 from the foul line.

Jordan was named to the All-American team as a senior in 1981 after averaging a triple-double of 29.2 points, 11.6 rebounds, and 10.1 assists per game as a senior. Jordan also joined his school's 1,000-point club in his senior year, scoring 1,165 points. Jordan, on the other hand, wasn't finished with high school basketball, as he played in a few of national all-star games. Jordan was a member of the United team that defeated Capital 91-85 in the McDonald's Capital Classic in Landover, Maryland on March 26, 1981. Jordan would finish with 14 points after making six of his twelve field goals in a contest that also featured names like Patrick Ewing and Lorenzo Gill on the opposing side.

Jordan, on the other hand, would be selected to participate in the annual All-American game in Wichita, Kansas, just a few days later. It was a sort of consolation game for Jordan, who scored 30 points on 13 of 19 field goals (68.4%), and was named the tournament's Most Valuable Player after making the final two free throws with 11 seconds left to give the East a 96-95 victory over the West. Jordan was a member of a South All-Star squad that competed in the National Sports Festival in Syracuse, New York from July 25 to 29 before going on to play college basketball. Jordan's side went 2-2 in the four games, with Jordan scoring 18 points in the South's 94-93 victory over the East on July 26, 1981.

Jordan was also a baseball player in high school, when he went 45 innings without allowing a run. His abilities drew interest from baseball teams at a number of Division I colleges, including Duke University, the University of South Carolina, Syracuse University, and the University of Virginia. Despite this, he was offered a scholarship at the University of North Carolina. He was one of the top prospects in the country, set to join a North Carolina Tar Heels team managed by famed college coach Dean Smith.

Jordan accepted the UNC scholarship and declared cultural geography as his undergraduate major, which is the study of culture and how it adapts to its geographical area as well as other aspects such as religion, language, government, and economy. While this was likely not an easy major to go through for eligibility, it's possible Jordan was expecting basketball would work out for him and that his academics were more of a hobby-like interest.

# Chapter 2: The University of North Carolina's College Years

## Freshman Year

Jordan had a fantastic year as a rising star from Wilmington, North Carolina, around 162 miles north of the University of North Carolina's Chapel Hill campus. It would be another 879 miles until the newest Tar Heel took his first step toward establishing himself as a clutch-shooter in important circumstances, beginning with his college debut in the Tar Heels' 74-67 season-opening triumph over the University of Kansas Jayhawks on November 28, 1981. Jordan missed his first shot as a collegiate basketball player, but he would make the next three, scoring 12 points on five of ten field goal attempts. Jordan would only be a Tar Heel for a few games before surpassing the 20-point mark with 22 points in the team's 78-70 win over Tulsa, which would be his season-high in scoring.

The Tar Heels concluded the regular season with a 32-2 record, 12-2 in the Atlantic Coast Conference, in Jordan's first year at Chapel Hill, and were ranked No. 1 in both the Coaches and Associated Press rankings. On March 7, 1982, the squad went three for three en route to a 47-45 conference championship win over third-ranked Virginia at the Greensboro Coliseum.

The Tar Heels' success continued throughout the 1982 NCAA National Championship tournament, which began with a second-round game against James Madison on March 13, 1982, in which Jordan made three of eight field goals (37.5 percent) and finished with six rebounds and one rebound in a 52-50 win. In addition to James Worthy's 15 points, Sam Perkins shone out among all players with 17 points and 10 rebounds on seven of thirteen shooting from the floor.

On March 19, 2013, they defeated Alabama in the Sweet 16 stage of the tournament, winning 74-69. The starting five were able to step up with minimal support, with two points coming from the bench. North Carolina's starters all scored in double digits, with Worthy and Matt Doherty both scoring 16 points, Perkins 15 points, and Jimmy Black 14 points. Jordan hit three of his six field goal tries (50%) and all five of his free throw attempts. In addition, he had three rebounds and three assists on the night.

Jordan would also score in double figures against the Villanova Wildcats, who were a third-seed with 22 victories, in North Carolina's Elite Eight encounter on March 21, 1982. Jordan scored 15 points in a 70-60 win over the Louisville Cardinals (23-10), Houston Cougars (25-8), and Georgetown Hoyas (33) in front of more than 50,000 fans at the Louisiana Superdome in New Orleans.

The Tar Heels defeated the University of Houston 68-63 on March 27, 2013. Future NBA legends Clyde Drexler and Hakeem Olajuwon were on this team.

Jordan's skills continued to improve in this game, as he made seven of 14 field goals and all four free throws to finish with 18 points, five rebounds, and two assists. Perkins, who hit 81.8 percent of his field goals (nine out of 11) and a perfect seven out of seven foul shots, was the only Tar Heel to score more than Jordan, with 25 points and 10 rebounds. On the other hand, on the Houston side of the floor, Drexler had 17 points while Olajuwon, a freshman, only had two points after making one of three field goals. However, it was early in his basketball career, and he had better performances in the years leading up to his NBA debut. However, the victory over Houston paved the way for a fantasy matchup between Georgetown and North Carolina.

In front of 61,612 people at the Louisiana Superdome in New Orleans, North Carolina trailed Georgetown 62-61 with 32 seconds left in the NCAA Championship game. Both teams featured players who would go on to have successful careers in the NBA a few years later. Patrick Ewing, another freshman, scored 23 points while shooting 10 of 15 (66.7 percent) from the field for the Hoyas, and Eric "Sleepy" Floyd added 18 points. The Tar Heels, on the other hand, possessed James Worthy, Sam Perkins, and Jordan, a brilliant rookie.

Down the stretch, no side led by more than a few points, and the Tar Heels were able to intercept an inbound pass. Dean Smith, the program's head coach, had never won a national championship in his 21 years in charge, after spending eight years as an assistant at

Kansas, Air Force, and North Carolina. He devised a play that would put the ball in Jordan's hands and trust him to make the shot if he was open.

Jordan was spotted on the left wing by teammate Jimmy Black, who hit the go-ahead jumper with 17 seconds left for the 63-62 advantage – probably the most critical of Jordan's 7 out of 13 field goals that night (53.8 percent). Georgetown subsequently turned the ball over, resulting in a foul on Worthy, who missed both of his free throw attempts. Fortunately, the Hoyas did not have any timeouts and were able to avoid a desperate heave. Smith's decision to pass the ball to Jordan, rather than Worthy or Perkins, was a wise one, and it proved to be a watershed moment in Jordan's basketball career.

Jordan had a solid freshman year at UNC, averaging 13.5 points per game in 34 games while shooting 53.4 percent from the floor. Jordan was named ACC Freshman of the Year for the 1981-1982 season, but his big moment came on March 29, 1982, when he played in the National Championship game at the Louisiana Superdome.

## Sophomore Year

Jordan averaged 20.0 points per game in 36 games as a sophomore, shooting over 53% from the floor. In addition, he raised his rebounding average from 4.4 per game as a freshman to 5.5 per game. The Tar Heels finished the season 28-8 and 12-2 in the Atlantic Coast Conference. However, after falling to North Carolina

State 91-84 in overtime on March 12, 1983, the Tar Heels were unable to repeat as ACC tournament winners. They were ranked ninth in the US and received a second-seed in the NCAA Tournament.

Following starting the season third in the polls, the team dropped to 15th after losses to St. John's University (78-74) and Missouri (64-60). UNC won 18 games in a row after a 3-3 start, and although losing three games in a row to Villanova, Maryland, and North Carolina State, they concluded the regular season with four straight ACC conference victories, including a 105-81 victory against Duke. The Tar Heels then competed in the ACC Conference tournament with the hopes of earning their conference's automatic bid to the National Championship. Things were looking up after a rout of the Clemson Tigers on March 11, 1983, but they were unable to maintain their momentum when they were defeated 91-84 in overtime by their in-state rivals, the North Carolina State Wolfpack, on March 12, 1983.

While the Tar Heels were unable to claim the ACC's one automatic entry to the championship tournament, they did receive an at-large ticket to the NCAA tournament, which is awarded to a team that finishes 26-7 against the difficult competition seen across the Atlantic Coast Conference.

The North Carolina Tar Heels were the second seed coming out of the East Region one year after capturing the national championship as the top seed overall. While being a favorite in their tournament opener seemed familiar, they were also up against a familiar adversary, James Madison University, which had just fallen by two points to North Carolina in the second round of the 1982 tournament. The ultimate result was identical to that of 1983. On March 19, 1983, Jordan finished the game with six out of eight field goals (75 percent) and made all three free throws from the foul line, despite the Tar Heels winning by a score of 68-49. He also contributed three rebounds and three assists to Perkins' team-leading 18 points.

The Tar Heels would go on to win the Sweet 16 against third-seeded Ohio State on March 25, 1983, by a score of 64-51. Jordan led the North Carolina blue and whites in scoring, but he struggled from the field, hitting only 5 of 15 shots (33.3 percent) while making seven of nine free throws. Jordan also had seven rebounds, five of which came while he was playing defense against the Buckeyes, who only made 44 percent of their total shots.

The Tar Heels were looking good at the perfect time, and analysts were beginning to second-guess their predictions from earlier in the month. However, on March 27, 1983, the Tar Heels were defeated by the University of Georgia, 82-77. Jordan showed a lot more of his potential despite the loss, making 11 out of 23 field goals (47.8%) and four out of five free throws for a final stat line of 26 points and six rebounds. Players like James Banks (20 points), Vern Fleming (18 points), and Gerald Crosby (18 points) led the Bulldogs.

In the next round, Georgia would lose to the eventual winners from North Carolina State, the same ACC squad that had kept the Tar Heels out of the conference championship earlier that month. Despite the fact that the squad did not win the National Championship, Jordan discovered that his shooting efficiency had improved slightly. Jordan would score 20 points per game (up from 13.5 points per game in his freshman season) with 5.5 rebounds, 2.2 steals, 1.6 assists, and slightly under one blocked shot a game if he shot 53.5 percent of his field goals. Jordan's individual statistics were excellent enough to earn him a berth on the first-team All-American squad.

### Junior Year

Jordan continued to play well in his junior year, earning a spot on the NCAA All-American First Team after averaging 19.6 points per game and shooting just over 55% from the field in a 31-game season. The Atlanta Tipoff Club would proclaim him the winner of the Dr. James Naismith Award for being the best male basketball player, an award named after the game's originator. Jordan was also honored by the Los Angeles Athletic Club with the John Wooden Award that same year. This award was established to recognize a renowned player and coach who won 11 NCAA championships.

Jordan scored 28 points right away in a non-conference game against Chattanooga at home on November 11, 1983, after making 13 of 17 field goals to lead the squad. Throughout the season, he would consistently score in the 20-point range, with 19 games in which he scored at least 20 points. Jordan's best individual performance occurred on February 2, 1984, in a 95-71 home victory over North Carolina State, when he scored 32 points on 12 of 18 field goals and eight of 11 foul line conversions. He'd get close to 30 points a few more times, notably in the team's 90-79 home win over Louisiana State on January 29, 1984, when he scored 29 points on a similar 12 for 18 shooting night and made all five free throw tries.

Jordan had a number of memorable moments during the season, including a breakaway slam with two seconds left after Perkins blocked a jumper in a 74-62 victory over Maryland on January 12, 1984. He glanced at the clock before putting the final nail in the coffin for the Terrapins with a windmill dunk that struck fear into the hearts of their ACC foes.

Jordan would also win the ACC Player of the Year award, the Adolph Rupp Trophy, and the US Basketball Writers Association's College Player of the Year as North Carolina finished with a 28-3 overall record and a 14-0 ACC record, and it appeared as if they would have a chance at the ACC's automatic berth into the NCAA National Championship tournament after defeating the Clemson Tigers 78-66 on March 8, 1984. After being beaten by long-time rival Duke in the semifinal round, 77-75, on March 10, 1984, North Carolina will once again fail to win the ACC Tournament. Being a top-ranked team in the AP and Coaches' rankings for the majority of the season almost always ensures a position in the championship tournament, which is why the Tar Heels were given the top seed in the East Regional.

On March 17, 1984, the Tar Heels bounced back from their ACC championship loss to Duke by defeating Temple 77-66 in the first round of the NCAA National Championship Tournament. Jordan scored 27 points in this game, one of four Tar Heels to score in double figures (Perkins,12; Kenny Smith, 11, and; Brad Daugherty, 10). Jordan's overall shooting abilities were on display as he made 11 of his 15 field goals (73.3 percent) and five of his seven free throws. Jordan also had six rebounds in the win over the Owls. It was a strong game to go to the Sweet 16, but North Carolina fell to the fourth-seeded Indiana Hoosiers in the second round, 72-68. Jordan didn't have his greatest game, as he only made 6 of 14 shots from the field, resulting in a total of 13 points for the game. Perkins, his teammate, had a near double-double with 26 points and nine rebounds.

Jordan would decide to bypass his senior season and join the 1984 NBA Draft, making it his final game with the Tar Heels. While Jordan's return to the Tar Heels would have made North Carolina one of the heavy favorites to win another national title in 1985, especially considering that he finished the season with 19.6 points per game, 5.3 rebounds, 2.1 assists, 1.6 steals, and 1.1 blocked shots.

The Houston Rockets selected Hakeem Olajuwon first overall, followed by Sam Bowie of the Portland Trail Blazers, and Jordan of the Chicago Bulls in third place.

Charles Barkley (fifth, Philadelphia 76ers), Alvin Robertson (seventh, San Antonio Spurs), Otis Thorpe (ninth, Kansas City Stars), Kevin Wills (eleventh, Atlanta Hawks), and John Stockton (sixteenth, Utah Jazz) were all members of the 1984 class, with the latter being someone Jordan would face a couple of times with championship implications.

Despite moving to the Windy City and embarking on probably one of the greatest NBA careers in history, he kept his UNC light blue and white. Jordan was named one of the most superstitious professional sportsmen by Men's Fitness magazine. During his 15-year career, the Chicago Bulls great is said to have worn his UNC shorts under his Bulls outfit in every game.

While Jordan would continue his basketball career in Chicago, it's worth mentioning that he would return to the University of North Carolina in Chapel Hill to finish his Bachelor's Degree in geography. He wasn't your typical North Carolina student, as he was making spectacular plays in the NBA while taking a range of collegiate classes, including Elementary Portuguese, Map Interpretation, and the Changing Human Environment, to name a few. He probably thought it was a good idea to finish his college education in case something happened that would cause a severe setback or bring his professional basketball career to a premature stop. That, however, would not be an issue, and he would not be forced to use his degree to get job.

# Chapter 3: The First Part of Michael's NBA Career

Before we go into Jordan's early years in the NBA, it's crucial to know that if Jordan had been selected in any other draft class in NBA history, he would have been the first overall pick instead of the third, as he was by the Chicago Bulls in 1984. The fact that the Houston Rockets and Portland Trail Blazers didn't need a point guard was the main reason Jordan's name was not mentioned. Some observers believed that the Rockets' selection of Hakeem Olajuwon and the Trail Blazers' selection of Sam Bowie was logical because both team lacked a big man to provide a commanding presence at center.

Stu Inman, Portland's general manager, stated multiple times that he thought Bowie was a superior overall choice than Jordan at the time. This was not because Bowie was superior; rather, they believed they already had someone with Jordan's skills in Clyde Drexler. Now, it's exceedingly unusual that anyone can precisely forecast someone's ability in any professional sport, let alone the NBA, before they even play their first game. As a result, it's difficult to dismiss Inman's remarks, although he'll almost certainly admit today that it was a bad mistake. Bowie spent ten seasons in the NBA, although he didn't do as well as many expected after graduating from the University of Kentucky. This was primarily due to a series of leg and foot ailments that derailed what could have been a promising career for the 7'1" center.

Michael Jordan's iconic No. 23 was worn by the Chicago Bulls against the Washington Bullets on October 26, 1984, in a 109-93 victory. He had 16 points, six rebounds, and seven assists in the game. He only hit five field goals out of 16 attempts, which was a good night for his debut NBA game. His veteran colleagues, such as Orlando Woolridge, who scored 28 points, and Quintin Dailey, who scored 25, led the squad. Jordan began to find his stride the following night, scoring 21 points in a 108-106 loss to the Milwaukee Bucks. He also had five rebounds and five assists. Woolridge led the Bulls in scoring with 29 points on the night.

Jordan would score 37 points two nights later against the Bucks in Chicago Stadium, converting 13 of 24 field goals (54.2 percent) and 11 of 13 free throws (84.6 percent) in the team's 116-110 victory on October 29, 1984. In one game, he had five assists and four rebounds. Woolridge, on the other side, would finish the game with 30 points. There was growing optimism that the partnership of Woolridge and Jordan would lead to grander things. Woolridge was also having his greatest season in Chicago, averaging nearly 23 points per game in 1984-1985, up from 19.3 points per game the previous season.

While Woolridge's numbers improved from his first three seasons after being drafted in 1981 out of nearby Notre Dame, Jordan was settling into his role as a shooting guard and second small forward to complement the rest of the Bulls' team. In the Bulls' 121-106 away victory over the New York Knicks on November 8, 1984, Jordan set a season best with 33 points after making 15 of 22 field goals (68.2%), eight rebounds, and five assists. That season-high number, though, wouldn't last long. Later in the season, in a 120-117 triumph over the San Antonio Spurs on November 13, 1984, he would break the 40-point barrier for the first time. Jordan recorded his first of many double-doubles in the NBA with 45 points, 10 rebounds, and four assists.

His Airness would score 45 points in a double-double with 11 assists as the Bulls upset the Cleveland Cavaliers, 112-108, on December 27, 1984, after making 20 of 33 field goals, which was the most shots he took during the regular season. On January 26, 1985, Jordan scored 45 points in a near tripledouble with 10 assists and eight rebounds in a 117-104 victory over the Atlanta Hawks. Jordan's solo performance came barely a week after he scored 42 points in a 119-113 loss to the New York Knicks on January 5, 1985. Jordan made 16 of 25 field goals for a 64 percent conversion rate and 10 of 11 free throws for an excellent offensive performance.

Jordan also scored 41 points in one of his first games, a 110-106 loss to Larry Bird and the Boston Celtics on February 5, 1985. Bird would finish with 27 points, nine rebounds, and seven assists in a team victory. After making 14 of 25 field goals (56 percent), 13 of 14 free throws, 12 rebounds, and seven assists, Jordan led all players. Jordan's best game of the season came a week later, when he beat the Detroit Pistons 139-126 at home on February 12, 1985. He hit 19 of 31 field goals (61.3 percent) and 11 of 13 foul shots for a total of 49 points. Jordan would add 15 rebounds and five assists to his stat line.

Jordan had 17 double-doubles during his remarkable rookie season, in addition to his high point totals. He'd also have three triple-doubles, which is difficult for any player in the NBA, let alone one in his first season. Jordan had 35 points, 15 assists, and 14 rebounds in a 122-113 win over the Denver Nuggets on January 14, 1985. A few months later, on March 1, 1985, Jordan had 21 points, 10 rebounds, and 10 assists in a 109-104 win over the New York Knicks, supporting Woolridge's team-leading 28 points. Jordan scored 32 points and made 11 of 25 shots from the field less than three weeks later, on March 17, 1985, to help the Bulls defeat the Milwaukee Bucks, 119-117. With 16 assists and 11 rebounds for a Chicago squad that had four players in double digits, three of whom scored more than 20 points (Jordan, 32, Quintin Dailey, 26, and Woolridges, 21), he demonstrated he was willing to share the ball for scoring opportunities.

During his rookie season in the NBA, he averaged 28.2 points per game, 6.5 rebounds, 5.9 assists, 2.4 steals, and nearly one block per game. Jordan was selected to participate in the 1985 NBA All-Star Game for the Eastern Conference on February 10, 1985, at the Hoosier Dome in Indianapolis, Indiana. Jordan took the court alongside Philadelphia's Julius Erving,

Boston's Larry Bird, and Detroit's Isiah Thomas in front of almost 43,000 basketball fans to face elite stars like the Los Angeles Lakers' Kareem Abdul-Jabbar and Magic Johnson. Jordan would play 22 minutes, making two of nine field goals and three of four free throws for a total of seven points, six rebounds, and two assists. The East, on the other hand, would lose 140-129 to the West.

In a season in which they finished third in the Central Division, Chicago went 38-44. They finished sixth in the Eastern Conference after losing more than half of their games. In a best-of-five series, the Bulls would lose 3-1 to the Milwaukee Bucks in the first round. Despite this, Jordan won the NBA Rookie of the Year title for his regular-season play. It also helped because he had been playing exceptionally well in the series against the division foe Bucks, which he had lost. Jordan would lead the squad with 23 points in the first game on April 19, 1985, while shooting only seven of 19 field goals (36.8%) in the team's 109-100 loss, where he converted nine of ten free throws while earning 10 assists, four rebounds, and three steals on defense.

Milwaukee would also win the second game, 122-115, on April 21, 1985.

Jordan had a stronger game on the court, hitting 9 of 17 field goals (52.9 percent) and 11 of 12 foul shots (11 of 12), while adding 12 assists, four rebounds, and two steals in 43 minutes. Jordan would add 35 more points in the 109-107 triumph in Game 3 in Chicago on April 24, 1985. Jordan led the Bulls to victory over the Bucks by making 12 of 26 field goals, 11 of 16 free throws, eight rebounds, seven assists, four steals, and one shot block. The series came to an end on April 26, 1985, when the Bucks defeated the Bulls 105-97 in Chicago. Jordan scored 29 points in this game, making 17 of 20 free throws. He, on the other hand, struggled on the field, making only 6 of 16 attempts (37.5 percent). Jordan had seven rebounds, five assists, three blocked shots, and two steals in Game 4 of the series.

Early on, he showed signs of being a star, and he would continue to do so throughout his career. Fans and experts could only guess what would happen next at the moment. Jordan had a lot of eyes on him when the team opened their season on October 25, 1985, hosting the Cleveland Cavaliers. While his rookie season was as strong as any Hall of Fame star in NBA history, Jordan had a lot of eyes on him when the team opened their season on October 25, 1985, hosting the Cleveland Cavaliers. In Chicago's 116-115 victory, Jordan made 13 of 16 field goals in 39 minutes, finishing with 29 points and 12 rebounds. Jordan and the Bulls would win 121-118 over the Detroit Pistons the next night, with Jordan scoring 33 points despite making only 9 of 24 field goals and 15 of 16 free throws.

Jordan's NBA sophomore season was cut short because he broke his foot in the third game, costing him 64 games. On March 1, 1986, he made his return in a 125-116 loss to Milwaukee. Jordan averaged only approximately 15 and a half minutes per game in his first six games back from the foot injury, converting only 35.9% of his field goal tries for an average of 14.7 points per game. Jordan would begin to reach his full potential on April 5, 1986, when he scored 30 points in the team's 102-97 victory over the Atlanta Hawks. In two of the team's final three regular-season games, he would score 30 points.

The Bulls nonetheless qualified for the playoffs despite the injury and a 30-52 record. Chicago received the Eastern Conference's eighth and final seed, just one game ahead of the ninth-place Cleveland Cavaliers and nearly nine games ahead of the sixth and seventh placed Washington Bullets and New Jersey Nets, both of which finished with 39-43 records. At the time, it was the league's fifth-worst record for a team entering the playoffs. Jordan was hitting his stride just in time for the first round series against the top-seeded Boston Celtics, who had the league's best record of 67 wins and 15 losses. Many people questioned whether or not the Bulls would be able to compete with the Celtics. While the Bulls were swept in the first round of the Eastern Conference Playoffs in three games in a best-of-five series, Jordan had several outstanding individual efforts that added to His Airness' early legacy.

While Boston would go on to win the series, Jordan demonstrated his abilities against a powerful Boston team that included Larry Bird, Kevin McHale, Robert Parish, Dennis Johnson, and Bill Walton, all of whom are Hall of Famers. Jordan led all players with 49 points in 43 minutes in the first game, which was played on the road against Boston on April 17, 1986. Jordan hit 18 of 36 field goals and 13 of 15 foul shots. The Celtics, on the other hand, would win 123-104. In a 135-131 loss, the Bulls forced the Celtics into two extra periods. Jordan was given plenty of chances, making 22 of 41 field goals (53.7 percent) and 19 of 21 free throws to finish with 63 points, six rebounds, five assists, three steals, and two blocked shots in 53 minutes. Six Boston players scored in double figures, led by Bird's 36 points, as the Celtics took a 2-0 series lead. On April 22, 1986, Boston won 122-104 in Chicago to complete the sweep. Jordan didn't have his finest game, but perhaps exhaustion was setting in as he only made 8 of 18 field goals (44.4 percent) for 19 points, 10 rebounds, and nine assists for a near triple-double. The Celtics, on the other hand, were too powerful, with McHale scoring 31 points, Ainge 20 points, and Bird 19 points, eight assists, and six rebounds.

Jordan fully recovered from his foot injury in time for the 1986-1987 season, when he played in all 82 games his route to becoming only the second player in NBA history to score 3,000 points in a single season, after Wilt Chamberlin – dubbed "Mr. 100." Jordan scored 37.1 points per game on 48.2 percent shooting from the field, which was a league high. Jordan had two games in which he scored 61 points. This happened against the Detroit Pistons on March 4, 1987, and again against the Atlanta Hawks on April 16, 1987. Jordan would go on to score 50 points in five more games, including 58 points in a 128-113 win over the New Jersey Nets on February 26, 1987, after hitting 16 of 25 from the field and 26 of 27 from the foul line. Jordan's offensive efficiency improved throughout the season, culminating in a field goal percentage of 70.4 in Chicago's 116-95 victory on April 12, 1987. Jordan scored 53 points on 19 of 27 shooting, his best percentage of the season, to go along with eight assists and four steals.

Jordan became the first player in NBA history to record 200 steals and 100 blocks in a season, which earned him a spot in the 1987 NBA All-Star Game, which was held on February 8, 1987 at the Kingdome in Seattle, Washington. Chicago finished with a 40-42 record, good enough for eighth place in the Eastern Conference. In the first round, though, they were swept by the Celtics once more. Jordan led the Bulls to a three-game winning streak over Boston, averaging 35.7 points, seven rebounds, six assists, and two steals per game.

If you thought Jordan had reached his scoring potential, think again. He would follow up that year with 35 points per game in the 1987-1988 season, the first of three seasons in which he would lead the league in steals and win the NBA Defensive Player of the Year award. Jordan had 13 double-doubles and two triple-doubles during the season, including a 36-point performance with 10 rebounds and 10 assists against the Detroit Pistons on January 16, 1988. Jordan would have his best offensive game on April 3, 1988, when he scored 59 points after making 21 of 27 field goals (77.8%) and 17 of 19 free throws (89.5 percent).

By defeating the Cleveland Cavaliers and winning the series 3-2, the Bulls advanced through the first round of the playoffs. Jordan scored more than 45 points per game on average, including 50 in Game 1 on April 28, 1988, and 55 in Game 1 on May 1, 1988. They were, however, eliminated by the Detroit Pistons after losing the best-of-seven series 4-1 to a Detroit squad headlined by Isaiah Thomas and the "Bad Boys," a bunch of rugged players. Jordan's scoring figures were not as high as they were versus Cleveland, but he still averaged 27.4 points per game. On May 12, 1988, he had his greatest game in Chicago's lone win, a 105-95 victory. Jordan would score 36 points on 14 of his 22 field goal tries while grabbing 11 rebounds.

Jordan continued to have big games throughout his early career, but he had yet to have a defining postseason moment. Despite displaying signs of being one of the top individual talents in all of professional sports, there were even questions about his capacity to ever win a title. Every young talent on the verge of becoming a legend, on the other hand, is bound to have a few buzzer-beater moments. Jordan has a slew of them, beginning with his first in Game 5 of the 1989 Eastern Conference Finals.

Jordan scored a jump jumper with six seconds left to give the Bulls a 99-98 lead, followed by a fast layup by Cleveland's Craig Ehlo with three seconds left to make it 100-99. A timeout was used by Chicago to create an inbound opportunity, and Jordan bounced off Ehlo and shoved another Cavalier to get free, where he took the inbound pass and shot from the foul line for a 101-100 victory. That night at the Coliseum in Richfield, Ohio, those two points were the most remembered of his 44 points.

Jordan jumping in joy and pumping his fist while jumping in the air as Ehlo fell to the ground in sorrow only a few steps away was the lingering image from that night. It was the first of many memorable moments Jordan delivered to Chicago fans. The Bulls and Cavaliers were division rivals in the Eastern Conference and played each other six times per season, thus beating Cleveland would be a typical occurrence. Jordan scored 69 points on the road in a 117-113 overtime triumph on March 28, 1990. Jordan finished with a 62.2 percent field goal percentage, 21-of-23 free throws, 18 rebounds, six assists, four steals, and a block for good measure.

The Bulls would eventually lose in seven games to the Detroit Pistons in the Eastern Conference Finals, a familiar hurdle. The Pistons would proceed to the NBA Finals the following season, so this would be the last time Chicago would play second fiddle to them. Three championships would be awarded in a row. The first was in 1990-1991, when the Bulls dominated with a 61-21 record, with Jordan averaging 31.5 points per game and hitting 53.9 percent of his field goals in 82 games. Jordan's best total performance came against the Golden State Warriors on December 27, 1990, when he scored 42 points, grabbed 14 rebounds, and dished out seven assists in a 128-113 victory. Jordan was named to the All-Star squad for the second time, this time helping the East upset the West, 116-114, in Charlotte, North Carolina, on February 10, 1991. Jordan finished with 26 points, five rebounds, and five assists on 10 of 25 shooting.

The Bulls were the Eastern Conference's top seed, and they began the season with a three-game sweep of the New York Knicks, which began on April 25, 1991, with Jordan scoring 28 points on 8 of 15 field goals, as well as six rebounds and six assists. On April 28, 1991, he scored another 26 points after making nine of 16 field goals in a more defensive struggle to upset the Knicks 89-79. Jordan would receive a lot more opportunities in the third game, making 14 of 28 from the field to end with 33 points, seven assists, and six steals for New York on April 30, 1991.

Jordan would continue to lead the Bulls into the conference semifinals against the Philadelphia 76ers, scoring 29 points in each of the Bulls' first two games. Despite Jordan leading everyone on the court with 36 points and converting on 20 of 34 field goals, Philadelphia would only win one game in the series, 99-97, on May 10, 1991. Jordan scored 38 points, grabbed 19 rebounds, and dished out seven assists in a 100-95 win over the Bulls in Game 4 on May 14, 1991, to help the Bulls capture the series. The Chicago Bulls were thus placed against the Detroit Pistons, a familiar rival who had previously kept them out of the NBA Finals.

This team, however, was not the same as in previous years, when the Bad Boys dominated the NBA. Jordan would score just under 30 points per game while connecting on 53.5 percent of his field goals as the Bulls swept their Central Division opponent in a four-game sweep. Jordan scored 35 points on 10 of 20 field goals and 13 of 14 free throws in a 105-97 victory over the Boston Celtics in the Eastern Conference Finals on May 21, 1991. Jordan then scored 33 points on 11 of 19 shooting from the field and 11 of 12 from the foul line in a 113-107 triumph on May 25, 1991, to give the Bulls a 3-0 series lead. On May 27, 1991, Chicago won 115-94 in Detroit, with Jordan scoring 29 points and Scottie Pippen adding 23 points and 10 assists.

Jordan improved his game in Game 2 of the 1991 NBA Finals against the Los Angeles Lakers, scoring 33 points, seven rebounds, 13 assists, two steals, and one block in a 107-86 victory. He also made 15 of 18 shots, including 13 in a row, for an 83.3 percent field goal percentage. Marv Albert's play-by-play call of "a terrific move by Michael Jordan!" as Jordan drove to the hoop and changed hands mid-air in what was considered a classic NBA Finals moment is remembered from this game. The victory gave the Bulls the momentum they needed to win the series 4-1 against a team headlined by Hall of Famers James Worthy and Magic Johnson. Jordan and the team are off to a good start in their first of two three-peat runs.

Jordan proceeded to prove that he was truly one of the best the next season, as the Bulls went 67-15 in the regular season and advanced to the championship series. They were up against Clyde Drexler and the Portland Trail Blazers this time. Jordan made an immediate impact in Game 1 with 35 points in the first half of a 122-89 victory at home. Jordan's incredible first half included six field goals from beyond the arc, the last of which became famous as Jordan went to the broadcast table and shrugged in disbelief. Chicago erupted on a 22-6 run to take a 66-51 advantage at halftime and never looked back.

While the Bulls lost the second game in overtime, 115-104, they won Games 3, 4, and 5 with 46 points in the series-clinching game in Portland, Oregon, where Chicago triumphed 119-106. Jordan made 14 of 23 shots from the field and 16 of 19 free throws.

Jordan scored 55 points in a 111-105 victory over the Phoenix Suns in Game 4 of the 1993 NBA Finals to put the Suns down 3-1. It was a tie for the second highest points in NBA Finals history at the time. Jordan only sat on the bench for 2 minutes out of the game's 48 minutes, making 21 of 37 shots with seven rebounds and four assists.

Jordan averaged 41 points per game in the six-game series, including 42 points in Game 2 (Chicago won 111-108) and 33 points in Game 6 (Chicago won 99-98), as the Bulls won their third title in a row, defeating the Suns 4-2. Jordan won his third NBA Finals Most Valuable Player title that year, having once again led the league in steals.

Jordan led the NBA for six consecutive seasons from 1987 to 1993, averaging 35.0 points per game, 32.5 points, 33.6 points, 31.5 points, 30.1 points, and 32.6 points per game. In 1991, he was also voted Sportsman of the Year. Jordan also won the NBA Slam Dunk Contest twice in his early career, in 1987 and 1988, when the Bulls were loaded with players like Scottie Pippen (who would go on to become a Hall of Famer), Bill Cartwright, Horace Grant, and John Paxson.

It was a dynasty that brought joy to a city that hadn't seen a championship squad in a long time. The most recent, at the time, was the 1985-1986 season, when the Chicago Bears won the National Football League's Super Bowl XX. Before that, the Blackhawks of the National Hockey League won the Stanley Cup in 1961. Since 1901, the Cubs have been without a championship in Major League Baseball. The White Sox had not fared much better after winning the World Series for the last time in 1917.

Jordan was nearing the end of his NBA career at the age of 29, and many wondered if the Bulls would ever be dethroned as champions. The answer would come the following season, but not in the way everyone had anticipated.

# Chapter 4: Baseball in Birmingham

Jordan was driving around Comiskey Park, the baseball stadium on Chicago's South Side, with Chicago Tribune columnist Bob Greene, the author of Hang Time: Days and Dreams with Michael Jordan, after the 1992-1993 NBA season and his third NBA title in a row. Jordan stated that he would be starting employment there soon. It was an intriguing declaration for the three-time NBA Finals MVP, who had just ended a season in which he averaged 39.3 points per game while leading the United States' "Dream Team" men's basketball team to a gold medal at the 1992 Olympic Games in Barcelona, Spain.

It wasn't the first time, though, that a professional athlete attempted to be a two-sport athlete. After winning the Heisman Trophy at Auburn University, NFL running back Bo Jackson spent three years with the Los Angeles Raiders from 1987 to 1990, rushing for 2,782 yards and 16 touchdowns. Jackson also had a career.250 batting average with 141 home runs and 415 RBIs as an outfielder for the Kansas City Royals (1986-1990) and the Chicago White Sox (1991, 1993).

Deion Sanders was an eight-time All-Pro linebacker in the National Football League, with more than 500 tackles, 50 interceptions, and 22 touchdowns in 13 seasons with five different teams, including the Dallas Cowboys. After being drafted by the New York Yankees, he had a nine-year part-time baseball career, which many baseball fans regard as America's club (much like the Cowboys in the NFL). On May 31, 1989, he made his Major League Baseball debut against the Seattle Mariners. Sanders finished his career with a.263 batting average, 39 home runs, and 168 RBIs.

So, if they were able to achieve success in two sports, why couldn't someone of Air Jordan's quality do the same? What else could a player with three titles and MVP awards in a row have to prove?

Jordan did not play for the Chicago Bulls at the start of the 1993-1994 season, but the team completed with a respectable 55-27 record and second place in the NBA Central Division before falling in the Eastern Conference Semifinals to the New York Knicks, 87-77. Scottie Pippen, Toni Kukoc, Horace Grant, and Steve Kerr, a rookie from the Orlando Magic, were among the players seeking to continue the momentum of a three-peat.

While the Bulls were attempting to catch the Atlanta Hawks and New York Knicks at the top of the Eastern Conference rankings, the man known as "Air Jordan" was practicing and playing at Ed Smith Stadium in Sarasota, Florida, arriving just days before his 31st birthday. Jordan wasn't your normal rookie, attending his first spring training session in the hopes of earning a spot on the 40-man roster for the six-month Major League Baseball season. Jordan had not played organized baseball since leaving the Laney High School team in Wilmington, North Carolina in March 1981. Jordan came in early and stayed late every day, demonstrating the same commitment and work ethic that earned him a three-time world champion in basketball.

The fact that the biggest star in basketball was playing baseball created quite a stir in Sarasota. The 8,500-seat stadium was packed with thousands of supporters. Crowds pressed up to the chain-link fence in the hopes of getting an autograph from Jordan, who did his best to make as many people happy as possible. It was an odd sensation for someone who had been the NBA's alpha male and was now trying to play someplace in the summer. Jordan had a difficult time getting to first base safely. Because of a fielder's choice, he was only able to do so after a half-dozen games.

Jordan did find a spot to play baseball that summer, but it wasn't in Comiskey Park in the South Side, as he had planned. He also didn't get picked to play at the next level with the Charlotte Knights, whose Triple-A club is only a four-hour drive from where he grew up and began playing sports. Instead, he was assigned to the Double-A Barons of the Southern League in Birmingham, Alabama. Jordan stood out among everyone that year as a 31-year-old amid teens and others in their early 20s since it was regarded a "prospects league" for younger players.

Jordan did get a chance to play in an exhibition game between the White Sox and the beloved Cubs at Wrigley Field in front of 35,000 fans who had come to watch their hero, who they had been following down the road at the Chicago Stadium, which was due to close in favor of the United Center. Jordan walked onto the field in the first inning and went two-for-five with two runs batted in, despite not being scheduled to start. After 10 innings, the game ended in a 4-4 tie, and the fans gave Jordan standing ovations for his performance in right field and at the plate, which was unusual because Chicago's baseball fan base did not have much to celebrate at the time.

Jordan's first visit to Wrigley Field as a baseball player came to an end when he returned to Birmingham, where he remained the entire season and appeared in 127 games, 119 of which he played in the outfield. Throughout the season, the baseball park in southern Alabama was packed with thousands of fans, many of whom traveled from all over the country. Not only for this team, but for minor league baseball in general, attendance records and item sales were definitely at all-time highs. Jordan's performance on the field, however, did not live up to the hype. On the opening weekend at home, he struck out seven times in his first nine at-bats. He only connected with the ball twice, resulting in a pop fly and an easy ground out to the infield.

In Birmingham, there was a report that Jordan had purchased an expensive new bus so that the squad could travel in style. While this was not the case, the team's bus provider did supply the Barons with a luxurious bus with reclining seats and a lounge in the back to help pass the time on lengthier road journeys between Nashville, Tennessee and Raleigh, North

Carolina, or Greenville, North Carolina and Orlando, Florida.

Jordan batted.260 in the final month of the season, raising his average to a pitiful. Only 88 hits were recorded in 436 at-bats, including 17 doubles and a long triple. He did, however, manage to steal 30 bases and cross home plate 46 times. When it comes to popular baseball statistics, the batting average of a player is usually the first thing that comes to mind. Jordan, on the other hand, hit three home runs and drove in 51 runs while drawing 51 walks and striking out 114 times.

Jordan would earn a "promotion" by being assigned to the Scottsdale Scorpions in the Arizona Fall League, where he batted.252 against some of the best prospects in professional baseball. While some, such as Barons manager Terry Francona, who would later coach the Boston Red Sox to numerous World Series titles, saw it as a triumph for Jordan, only a few White Sox executives did.

Jordan's #23 jersey was retired by the Bulls on November 1, 1994, in a ceremony that included the unveiling of The Spirit, a permanent sculpture outside the newly completed United Center. It's a bronze statue of Michael Jordan in his characteristic slam dunk position, which can be seen on a variety of Jordan merchandise such as sneakers and shirts.

The Bulls had a rough start to the 1994-1995 season when Horace Grant opted to quit the team and sign with the Orlando Magic. Meanwhile, Jordan was in Arizona, where he was rumored to be in talks to play for the White Sox at the Triple-A level. However, the strike that caused the end of the 1994 season to be postponed was still unresolved, and the owners were considering utilizing substitute players.

The Bulls needed aid as they approached February and the closing months of the regular season, as they were hanging around a.500 win-loss record. Jordan approached Jackson about returning before to spring training, and the two agreed that he would play 20 games with the Bulls while returning to spring training prior to the 1995 MBL season. Jordan, on the other hand, would not be staying for long.

Major league players were absent, prompting the players' union to enact a rule known as the Jordan Rule. A minor leaguer who plays in a game where admission is paid is deemed a strike breaker, according to the rule. The White Sox's owners pushed for Jordan to play preseason games in order to keep fans interested in the team without the regular major league talent. Jordan decided it was better to step away from the situation. As a result, on March 3, 1995, Air Jordan retired from baseball and returned to the NBA as a member of the Chicago Bulls.

# Chapter 5: The Second Part of Michael's NBA Career

Jordan's return to the NBA was greeted with rapturous applause not only among Chicago Bulls fans, but also across the United States and around the world.

During a press conference at the time, even US President Bill Clinton joked that Jordan's comeback to professional basketball had improved the country's unemployment rate by one. Local and national news outlets followed his return to practice with his customary teammates, with whom he hadn't played in almost a year. In addition, instead of playing at Chicago Stadium, the Bulls are now based in the United Center.

Jordan's debut game, on March 19, 1995, culminated in an overtime loss as the Bulls lost 103-96 on the road to the Indiana Pacers. Jordan had arrived late for the 1994-1995 season. He struggled offensively, making only 7 of 28 field goals for 19 points, six rebounds, six assists, and three steals. After spending more than a year swinging a bat at a ball instead of trying to toss it into a basket, it may be regarded the game where he shook off some of the basketball rust.

Jordan led all scorers with 27 points in Chicago's 124-107 road victory over the Boston Celtics on March 22, 1995, shooting 9-of-17 from the field. A week later, Chicago was relieved to see Jordan return, especially during a 113-111 victory over the New York Knicks at Madison Square Garden, where Jordan scored 55 points in front of more than 19,000 fans in his fifth game back from his basketball hiatus. Jordan made 21 of 37 shots from the field. It was a sign that he was finally shaking off the rust and reclaiming his "Air Jordan" moniker.

Jordan's numbers appeared similar to his past 14 seasons, with an average of 39.0 points per game, helping the Bulls win 12 of their final 14 games to end with a 47-35 record, good for third place in the Central Division and fifth place in the Eastern Conference. The Bulls went on to win the best-of-five first-round series against the fourth-seeded Charlotte Hornets, including a 108-100 overtime triumph on April 28 in Charlotte, where Jordan had 48 points, nine rebounds, and eight assists in 47 minutes on the floor.

Jordan would score 32 points in Game 2 (a 106-89 defeat), 25 points in Game 3 (a 103-80 victory), and 24 points in Game 4 (a 85-84 series-clinching victory). However, Chicago would go on to suffer in the second round, losing 4-2 to the Orlando Magic. Jordan, on the other hand, had standout performances with 38 points in Game 2, 40 points in Game 3, and 39 points in Game 5.

Jordan and the Bulls would return to form with a 72-win season and only 10 losses, despite missing the NBA Finals. He averaged 30.4 points per game and shot nearly 50% from the field, including 42.7 percent from outside the three-point line, to lead his whole squad with 2,491 points in all 82 games. He hit the 30-point and 40-point thresholds numerous times in a number of games. In a home win over the Detroit Pistons, he scored 53 points while adding 11 rebounds, two assists, and six steals on defense.

Jordan benefited from a great supporting cast that featured Scottie Pippen, who served as a sort of second in command, as well as Steve Kerr, Toni Kukoc, and Dennis Rodman. Rodman, who was noted for his colorful and patterned hair, was a member of the Detroit Pistons during Jordan's early years in the late 1980s, when the "Bad Boy" era hindered the Bulls from winning titles.

It was the first of three consecutive seasons in which Jordan won the NBA scoring title, as well as the start of another three-peat for the Bulls. The Bulls swept the Miami Heat in three games, then went on to win four of five games against the New York Knicks and then sweep the Orlando Magic. The Bulls were able to overcome the Seattle Supersonics in six games, despite Jordan's 27.3 point average. On June 9, 1996, in Seattle's Key Arena, he led Chicago to a 108-86 victory in Game 3 of the series, earning him the MVP award. Jordan had 36 points, five assists, three rebounds, and two steals in the game.

The Bulls won 69 games the following season, and Jordan won the NBA scoring title for the second time, averaging 29.6 points per game over the course of the 82-game regular season. Jordan had two games where he scored 50 points or more. On November 6, 1997, he had 50 points, six rebounds, a steal, and a block against Miami. On January 21, 1997, he topped that effort with 51 points on 18-of-30 field goals, four rebounds, four assists, and two steals at home against the New York Knicks.

Jordan scored 55 points with seven rebounds against the Washington Bullets in the 1997 NBA playoffs, shooting 22-of-35 from the field and a perfect 10-for-10 from the foul line. His most important game of the season, though, was one in which he did not reach the 40- or 50-point mark. On June 11, 1997, at the Delta Center in Salt Lake City, Jordan's intensity shone in Game 5 of the NBA Finals against the Utah Jazz.

Jordan was playing with a stomach bug, which was plainly evident both to fans in attendance and on live television, in a game dubbed "the Flu Game" by NBA experts. Despite clear signs of illness and exhaustion, he refused to allow a minor illness prevent him from taking a key 3-2 series lead by defeating the Jazz 90-88. Jordan finished with 38 points, seven rebounds, five assists, three steals, and one block in 44 of the game's 48 minutes of action. After a solid win with a Hall of Fame performance from someone who wasn't even 100 percent healthy, the Bulls rode the momentum to win the sixth game of the series against Utah, 90-86, at the United Center, with Jordan finishing with a double-double of 39 points and 11 rebounds. Jordan was named NBA Finals MVP for the second year in a row.

With a 62-20 record in the 1997-1998 NBA season, the Bulls were once again on top of the Central Division and Eastern Conference, en route to three consecutive NBA Championships. Jordan started all 82 regular-season games for the third consecutive season, averaging 28.7 points, 5.8 rebounds, 3.5 assists, and 1.7 steals per game. The Bulls swept the New Jersey Nets in three games in the first round then defeated the Charlotte Hornets 4-1 in the second round of the Eastern Conference playoffs.

The Indiana Pacers, led by Reggie Miller, threw Chicago for a loop, forcing the Bulls to play seven games before winning the Eastern Conference title. Jordan had 31 points, 41 points, 30 points, 28 points, 29 points, 35 points, and 28 points in the seven-game series, respectively. His winning streak continued against his "Dream Team" teammates John Stockton and Karl Malone, with Chicago defeating the Utah Jazz 4-2 for the second year in a row.

Jordan just had one rebound and one assist in an 87-86 win in Game 6. He shot 42.9 percent from the field. With less than a minute left, he was able to decrease Utah's lead to one point. Jordan then scored with 5.2 seconds left in the game after forcing a turnover by grabbing the ball from Malone's hands. The Jazz were unable to retaliate because their final shot was missed. Jordan scored 45 points in the NBA Finals to give the Bulls their sixth championship in eight seasons, cementing his status as the greatest player in NBA history with his sixth NBA Finals MVP award to go along with his previous awards and achievements.

Things seemed to be changing in Chicago, just as they had at the end of the first three-peat. Head coach Phil Jackson's contract was up for renewal, and Scottie Pippen (trade) and Dennis Rodman (signing with the Los Angeles Lakers) were expected to depart. The NBA was also nearing the end of a player lockout imposed by the owners. Jordan's second retirement came on January 13, 1999, as a result of all of these issues. Jordan became a part owner and President of Basketball Operations for the Washington Wizards a year later.

Meanwhile, under new head coach Tim Floyd, the Bulls finished 13-37 in the lockout-shortened season, leading a team that featured only a few recognizable faces from the previous season — Toni Kukoc, Bill Wennington, and Ron Harper. The Bulls' fortunes did not improve the next season, as they won only 17 games in 1999-2000 and did not have another winning season until the 2004-2005 season, when they finished 47-35. Since Jordan's second three-peat, the Bulls have not won an NBA championship, much like the team had not won any before to Jordan's first three-peat.

Jordan chose to stay in the District of Columbia rather than return to the Chicago Bulls. With six championships, six NBA Finals MVP trophies, 11 All-Star Game selections, and five regular season MVP honors in 13 seasons in the red, black, and white, it seemed like the right moment to hang up his basketball shorts and call it a career.

If there's one thing we've learned about "His Airness," it's that you can't totally predict what Jordan will do next, nor can you truly know if he will retire altogether.

# Chapter 6: The Third Part of Michael's NBA Career

Some of the top athletes in professional sports go on to coach or work in the front office of the teams for which they once played. Jordan, on the other hand, desired to become a partial owner and participate in some type of NBA decision-making. As a result, his return to the league began with him wearing a suit rather than a basketball gear — at least not straight away.

On January 19, 2000, Jordan returned to the NBA as a part owner and President of Basketball Operations for the Washington Wizards. He was in charge of making personnel choices, such as drafting rookie players and managing both current players who might be entering the free agent market and those who are currently looking for a new team to replace those who are leaving.

Jordan's performance as a basketball executive was met with mixed reviews. He was able to trade Juwan Howard, Obinna Ekezie, and Calvin Booth to the Dallas Mavericks for Hubert Davis, Courtney Alexander, Christian Laettner, Loy Vaught, and Etan Thomas, with $3 million thrown in, for Hubert Davis, Courtney Alexander, Christian Laettner, Loy Vaught, and Etan Thomas. However, Kwame Brown, a high school star who failed in his own right and was traded by the Wizards after only four seasons, was Jordan's first pick in the 2001 NBA Draft.

Despite claiming in January 1999 that he was 99.9% confident he would never play another NBA game again, in the summer of 2001, he expressed interest in making a comeback. The only difference is that he would not be donning the Chicago Bulls' red and black this time. Instead, he donned the Wizards' blue and gold. It was comparable to Mario Lemieux's predicament as a player/owner of the Pittsburgh Penguins in the National Hockey League the previous winter.

The Wizards were overjoyed to have someone of Jordan's stature, which he brought with him from Chicago - six championships and six NBA Finals MVP trophies to be exact. The 2000-2001 season ended with a 19-63 record for Washington. After that, after only one season, Leonard Hamilton was fired. Howard was dealt to Dallas as a result of his poor play, averaging only 12.9 points per game in 54 games prior to the move. Richard Hamilton, who averaged 18 points, 3.1 rebounds, 2.9 assists, and one steal per game in his third season in the NBA, was given more starting time after averaging 18 points, 3.1 rebounds, 2.9 assists, and one steal per game.

Jordan spent the off-season leading up to the 2001-2002 season exercising and holding various invitation-only camps in Chicago with other players. For the 2001-2002 season, he also hired Doug Collins as the Wizards' head coach. During Jordan's early years in the NBA, he was the Bulls' head coach. All of this was a foreshadowing of his third season in the league, which he revealed on September 25, 2001. He also declared that he would contribute his active player pay to a relief effort for the victims of the terrorist attacks on September 11, 2001.

Despite the changed colors, Jordan hit the floor on October 30, 2001 with 19 points, five rebounds, six assists, and four steals in a 93-91 loss to the New York Knicks. Jordan would score 31 points on the road against the Atlanta Hawks a few days later, nearly completing a double-double with nine assists.

Jordan's first double-double occurred against the Seattle Supersonics on November 11, when he had 16 points and 12 rebounds in a 99-84 win at home. Jordan finished the regular season with averages of 22.9 points, 5.7 rebounds, and 5.2 assists per game, for a total of eight double-doubles. Jordan struggled with his three-point shooting in his first season with the Wizards, not making a shot from beyond the arc until the Wizards' November 16 game against the Utah Jazz, in which he scored 44 points.

Jordan had a mix of excellent and bad games this time around. Jordan scored 51 points and set a franchise record with 24 first-quarter points and 34 points at halftime in a 107-90 victory over the Hornets at the MCI Center in Washington, DC, a few nights after having his worst game of his career, scoring a career-low six points against the Indiana Pacers and ending a streak of 866 games of 10 points or more. Jordan made 21 of 38 field goals and 9 of 10 free throws. In 38 minutes on the court, he also had seven rebounds and four assists.

It was his 39th 50-point game of the season and his first since scoring 55 points in a playoff game against Washington for Chicago. Jordan moved to the right, around Charlotte's Jamaal Magloire, dangled in the air for a long time, and drew the foul while hitting a 14-footer off the glass. This was a sign that, despite his advanced age, he still had some useful skills. Jordan was one of the players that didn't exhibit his age in this game. Due to torn cartilage in his right knee, his season was cut short after only 60 games. It was the fewest games he had played since returning to the NHL late in the 1994-1995 season after his first retirement (17 games).

After only 19 victories the previous season, the Wizards improved their record to 37-45 in 2001-2002. Despite this, the team was unable to make the NBA playoffs, finishing fifth in the Eastern Conference standings, five games behind the Indiana Pacers. It was Jordan's first season without making the playoffs, and it felt strange to the future Hall of Famer. Even in their early years with the Bulls, they would at least make it to the first round of the playoffs.

Jordan had one 50-point game, four games with at least 40 points, 11 games with at least 30 points, 20 games with at least 20 points, and another 19 games with double digits by the end of the 2001-2002 season. He did, however, go five games without scoring at least ten points.

It was also the first time Jordan had missed to start a game since the 1986-87 season, when he started all 82 games and appeared in 742 games as a Chicago Bull. In his comeback to the Chicago Bulls in the 1994-1995 season, he started all 17 games he was able to play before starting all 82 games in each of his final three seasons with the team from 1995 to 1998.

Jordan would play in all 82 games for the 2002-2003 season, starting 67 of them. That season, he was the only Washington Wizard to do so. Jordan averaged 20 points per game, 6.1 rebounds, 3.8 assists, and 1.5 steals despite being 40 years old at the time. In 42 games, he scored 20 points or more, nine times passing the 30-point barrier, and three times passing the 40-point mark. During the Wizards' 89-86 win over the New Jersey Nets on February 21, 2003, Jordan became the first 40-year-old to score more than 40 points in a game (43) in the NBA. Jordan had one of his best performances of the season when the Wizards beat the Pacers 107-104 on January 4, 2003, when he had a double-double with 41 points and 12 rebounds, four assists, and three steals.

Jordan was named to his 14th and last NBA All-Star Game, which was held on February 9, 2003 at the Philips Arena in Atlanta. He then passed Kareem Abdul-Jabbar as the all-time leading scorer in the event's history after scoring 20 points in a 155-145 double overtime loss to the West. Jordan scored 262 points in 14 All-Star Game appearances during his career, a record that has since been surpassed twice. Kobe Bryant of the Los Angeles Lakers presently has 280 points, while LeBron James is second with 278 points, putting Jordan in third place all-time in the All-Star voting.

Jordan's final game was on April 16, 2003 in Philadelphia, where he only scored 13 points and was benched with just over four minutes left in the third quarter and the team behind by one. The audience began chanting "We want Mike!" at the start of the fourth quarter. With 2:35 left in the game, they were able to persuade Collins, the head coach, to allow him to return. Jordan earned a standing ovation from everyone in the grandstand and on the court — almost 21,000 people in total – when he returned to the bench after a few minutes.

It was a year of tributes for Jordan, who officially announced that this would be his final season in the NBA — and it was true this time. On January 24, he earned a standing ovation at his former home court of Chicago's United Center, where he only scored 11 points in a 104-97 loss. While the Chicago Bulls retired his #23 number, the Miami Heat retired their #23 jersey on April 11 before the Wizards won 91-87, with Jordan leading all players with 25 points.

Jordan drew tens of thousands of fans at home during his final NBA season, averaging more than 20,000 at the MCI Center in Washington, DC, and more than 19,000 at any given arena around the country. Despite Jordan's inability to lead Washington to the playoffs, something he did in each of his 13 seasons in Chicago, the Wizards were the second most watched team in the NBA.

# Chapter 7: Olympic Gold Standard

Dr. James Naismith, a native of Almonte, Canada, invented basketball in 1891 at a YMCA in Springfield, Massachusetts. So it's no surprise that the United States leads the International Basketball Federation (FIBA) global rankings with 14 golds, two bronzes, and one silver – which they refused to accept following a contentious 51-50 loss to the Union of Soviet Socialist Republics (USSR), now known as Russia.

Jordan has two gold medals from the Summer Olympics, the first coming after his junior year at North Carolina as one of several collegiate programs around the state and as one of the last amateur teams for the United States Men's Olympic basketball team to win a gold medal.

While they were considered amateur undergraduate athletes at the time, the team included some of the best players of the day, including seven-foot Patrick Ewing of Georgetown University, Jordan's UNC colleague Sam Perkins, and University of Arkansas' Alvin Robertson. Jordan was regarded one of the top two performances at the Indiana University trials in Bloomington, Indiana in April of that year, along with Auburn junior Charles Barkley — who ended up being one of the last cuts owing to his personality not meshing with Indiana head coach Bob Knight. John Stockton and Terry Porter were among those who made the cut, and both went on to have successful NBA careers.

Jordan's first taste of international basketball competition was not at the 1984 Summer Olympics in Los Angeles. Jordan was a member of the USA Amateur Team after his freshman year at North Carolina, and he played on a tiny European Tour that began with two losses against the Europe All-Stars on June 18, 1982 (111-92), and June 20, 1982 (111-92). (103-88). The US squad then went on to win two of three games against Yugoslavia's national team between June 23 and June 27 of the same year.

Jordan was a member of the United States national team that competed in the 1983 Pan American Games in Caracas, Venezuela, which began in August 1983. The Americans would go undefeated, with Jordan scoring double digits in all but one game, a 78-65 victory over Venezuela on August 20, 1983. Jordan scored 27 points against Brazil in a 72-69 victory on August 16, 1983, and 24 points against Argentina in an 88-68 victory on August 25, 1983.

Fast forward to the Summer Olympics in Los Angeles, where the US team went undefeated in the tournament, averaging 95.4 points per game while holding their opponents to a 63.3 point per game average. Jordan led Team USA in scoring with an average of 17.1 points per game, followed by Chris Mullin (11.6), Ewing (11.0), and Steve Alford (10.0). (10.3). Jordan also averaged one and a half steals per game, with three against Uruguay on August 1, 1984, two against France on August 3, 1984, and three against Spain on August 4, 1984, and three more in the gold medal game on August 10, 1984.

On July 29, 1984, the United States began with a 97-49 thrashing of China, with Jordan scoring 14 points on five of eight field goals. On July 31, 1984, Jordan would follow up with 20 points on 10 of 17 field goals as the United States upset Canada, 89-68, in one of their closest games. On August 6, 1984, the United States defeated a difficult West German squad, 78-67, in the quarterfinal stage, after three blowout wins against Uruguay (104-68), France (120-62), and Spain (101-68). Jordan had 15 points, four rebounds, three assists, and one steal in the game. Jordan would add 13 more points, four rebounds, three assists, and one steal in the 78-59 semifinal victory over Canada on August 8, 1984.

Jordan led all players with 20 points in the gold medal game, shooting 9 of 15 from the field with two assists and three steals in a 96-65 victory for the United States over Spain on August 10, 1984. Jordan's success in the 1984 Olympics is highly likely to have boosted his worth in the forthcoming NBA Draft. After all was said and done, he was drafted third overall by the Chicago Bulls and went on to become the league's next youthful sensation.

Because the International Basketball Federation (FIBA) did not have the rules in place to allow professional basketball players from the NBA and other smaller leagues around the world to represent their country at the 1988 Olympic Games in Seoul, South Korea, Jordan and others would not be able to compete.

The future USA men's basketball team would still be made up of collegiate all-stars and would be one of the few squads without any NBA players. The squad was led by Georgetown head coach John Thompson to a 7-1 record, but they were upset by the Soviet Union, 82-76. The United States would come back to defeat Australia for the bronze medal, 78-49.

Team USA underwent some changes as a result of not winning the gold, or even playing in the gold medal game. There were more requests for professionals to be allowed to play for their country, a move that FIBA's Borislav Stankovi had pushed for for years. In 1989, it was finally approved by a vote of all members of the organization, despite the fact that the United States and Russia voted against it. When USA Basketball was asked to contribute players for the 1992 roster, NBA officials were concerned since no one could have predicted the cultural phenomenon that the team would become. The 1988 Summer Olympic Games were the final time the men's squad did not include current NBA players, and the "Dream Team" was constructed in preparation for the 1992 Summer Olympics in Barcelona, Spain.

The first roster was released on September 21, 1991. Jordan and Bulls teammate Scottie Pippen were among those in attendance, as were Utah Jazz Karl Malone and John Stockton, Magic Johnson of the Los

Angeles Lakers, Larry Bird of the Boston Celtics, and Charles Barkley of the Philadelphia 76ers. David Robinson, who was a member of the US Naval Academy at the time and is now a member of the San Antonio Spurs, was the only returning standout from the 1988 squad.

With that much star power on one roster, the team became known as the Dream Team, which American sports journalists regard as the finest sports team ever assembled. Several corporate sponsors, including McDonald's, Coca-Cola, and Kellogg's, expressed interest in using the team in their ads. Many people, however, had to be turned away.

After realizing he had HIV in November 1991, Johnson was forced to leave the team, and the vacated place was filled by Isaiah Thomas of the Detroit Pistons and Clyde Drexler of the Portland Trail Blazers. Drexler and Christian Laettner of Duke University were joined on May 12, 1992.

On June 24, 1992, they were defeated in a scrimmage game against an all-star team of college basketball's best, which included Bobby Hurley, Chris Webber, Grant Hill, and Penny Hardaway (the latter two would subsequently represent Team USA for the 1996 Olympics). After Team USA lost 62-54, head coach Chuck Daly began limiting Jordan's playing time and making additional adjustments after underestimating the competition. Later, assistant coach Mike Krzyzewski stated that the head coach intentionally tossed the game in order to teach the NBA players that they were not unstoppable.

The 1992 Tournament of the Americas, currently known as the FIBA Americas Championships, was held in the Memorial Coliseum in Portland, Oregon, from June 27 to July 5. The United States swept their group with comfortable wins, including a 136-57 victory over Cuba on June 28. Jordan only scored six points, second lowest to Barkley's four, demonstrating the Dream Team's genuine depth. With an unblemished record, the United States advanced to the semifinals, where they were defeated 119-81 by Puerto Rico. The United States then defeated Venezuela by a score of 127-80.

It was little surprise that the United States would repeat their 1988 gold-medal performance at the Olympics, where they went undefeated. In his career, both in the NBA and in Olympic contests, the younger Jordan put a premium on his defensive performance. Jordan recorded eight thefts in USA's opening game against Angola on July 26, 1992, as the "Dream Team" had ten players combine for 30 steals – possibly the main reason why Angola scored only 48 points in a 116-48 triumph. Jordan got five thefts in the USA's 122-81 semifinal win over Spain on August 2, 1992, and another six in the 127-76 semifinal win over Lithuania on August 6, 1992, to go along with his 21 points on 9-of-18 shooting.

Jordan even had a double-double in their 111-68 triumph over Germany on July 29, 1992, with 15 points and 12 assists to go along with four steals and two blocks on defense. On August 8, 1992, Jordan led the United States with 22 points in the gold medal game, a 117-85 victory over Croatia. Jordan scored his points by completing 10 of 14 field goals in the game. He also added two more steals to his tally. Squad USA was not only a great team in athletics, but also one of the most recognizable. In 2010, the squad was eventually inducted into the Naismith Memorial Basketball Hall of Fame.

Jordan told the media after winning a gold medal after his first two NBA championships that the biggest benefit for him was knowing his teammates' flaws – just in time for the start of the 1992-1993 NBA season. Not that he needed the extra scouting report because he would go on to defeat Barkley in the NBA Finals and later defeat teammates Malone and Stockton in back-to-back NBA Finals as the Bulls defeated the Jazz.

Jordan's impact as a part of the "Dream Team," in addition to his impact in the NBA, would help expand the NBA's global fame, with so much interest in the games in Barcelona, resulting in an increase in the number of international players in the league. NBA rosters contained 23 players from 18 nations other than the United States at the start of the 1991-92 season. In fact, only a few years ago, there were 74 participants representing 35 countries.

Since the "Dream Team" won four gold medals (1996, 2000, 2008, and 2012) and one bronze medal (1996,

2000, 2008, and 2012), USA Basketball has attracted some of the top NBA players (2004). Kyrie Irving, Klay Thompson, John Wall, and DeMarcus Cousins are just a few of the current NBA players. Dwayne Wade, Jason Kidd, Kobe Bryant, Carmelo Anthony, and LeBron James are among the other athletes who have worn the red, white, and blue.

# Chapter 8: Michael Jordan's Past, Present, and Future

Jordan's time with the Wizards was over, and not just on the court, after 15 years in the NBA with three different teams and three different coaches. Jordan was sacked as the President of Basketball Operations by team owner Abe Pollin on May 7 due to the previously reported mixed outcomes in the front office with the trade of Richard Hamilton for Jerry Stackhouse. Jordan kept himself busy for the following few years by participating in celebrity golf tournaments, starting his own clothing line, and even owning a professional motorcycle racing team in the American Motorcyclist Association. Jordan, on the other hand, bought a minority investment in the Charlotte Bobcats in 2006 and became the Managing Member of Basketball Operations, overseeing the team's basketball operations. Jordan's company, MJ Basketball Holdings, would eventually become the primary owner of the Bobcats, making him the first former player to possess a controlling stake in an NBA team.

The Jordan-owned Bobcats had their finest season in franchise history in 2013-2014, going 43-39 and earning a playoff berth, but were swept in four games by the Miami Heat. Since then, he has assisted in the renaming of his home state's premier professional team, the New Orleans Hornets, to the Pelicans for the

2013-2014 season. Before moving from North Carolina to Louisiana in 2002, the Pelicans were known as the Charlotte Hornets. Jordan was instrumental in convincing the NBA to allow Charlotte to recover their name and records from 1988 through 2002. Long-time basketball fans in the Charlotte area were ecstatic to dust up their 1980s and 1990s purple and teal uniforms.

While Jordan's career as a club owner and President has had its ups and downs, many basketball analysts consider him to be one of, if not the greatest, players to ever grace the court. It's not every day that the city of Chicago honors an athlete with a bronze statue depicting an outstanding moment from their career outside of a stadium. But that is what Jordan's successes have meant to the Windy City, which also has particular locations for other sports giants such as Chicago Bears' Walter Payton and Mike Ditka, and Chicago Cubs' Ernie Banks and Ron Santo. Chicago is a city that prides itself on having some of the top athletes in their respective sports. Jordan is their basketball legend, having won six championships in a decade — a feat accomplished by only a few sportsmen and teams.

Jordan scored 32,292 points in his career, which ranks fourth all-time after Kareem Abdul-Jabbar (38,387), Karl Malone (36,928), and Kobe Bryant (36,928). (32,482). Jordan even eclipsed Wilt Chamberlain, who set a record with 100 points in a 169-147 win over the New York Knicks on May 2, 1962 as a member of the Philadelphia Warriors. Jordan also has 6,672 rebounds, 5,633 assists, 2,514 steals, and 893 defensive blocks in his 15-year career.

Jordan finished his career with ten All-NBA First Team selections from 1987 through 1993 and 1996 to 1998, along with one Second Team selection in 1985, in addition of six NBA championships and NBA Finals Most Valuable Player accolades (1991-93, 1996-98). Jordan was named to the All-Defensive First Team nine times for his ability to steal the ball while simultaneously scoring (1988-1993, 1996-98). He won the game's MVP award three times in his 14 All-Star Game appearances, in 1988, 1996, and 1998. He also won two Olympic gold medals, in 1984 and 1992.

Jordan's legacy, though, extended beyond the basketball court. One of the most significant was Nike's marketing decision to give Jordan his own shoe brand. When discussing about Jordan's superior skills on the basketball court, movie director and producer Spike Lee once quipped in one of the earliest ads for Nike's Air Jordan sneakers, "It's gotta be the shoes," in one of the oldest commercials from the 1980s.

Jordan signed a five-year deal with Nike, earning $500,000 per year plus royalties, shortly after being picked by the Chicago Bulls in 1984. The sneakers, which featured a silhouette of Michael Jordan's famed slam dunk from the free throw line, became a must-have for basketball players and fans in the 1980s and 1990s. The Jordan Brand is a part of Nike, and his current arrangement with the shoe business brings in more than $60 million in royalties alone. Jordan's sneakers are still a top seller at shoe stores today, and they compete with LeBron James' shoes on a regular basis.

Many people who grew up in the 1990s remember the movie Space Jam, which starred Bugs Bunny, Daffy Duck, Porky Pig, and Tweety Bird, in addition to sneakers and basketball clips. Bill Murray, Muggsy Bogues, Patrick Ewing, Shawn Bradley, Larry Johnson, Danny Ainge, and fellow Hall of Famer Larry Bird all had cameo cameos in the 1996 film, which was released in theaters. Although the film did not receive a positive review, the tale was entertaining, especially when you consider Jordan's role in preventing the cartoon characters from becoming inmates of an intergalactic theme park by winning a basketball game. Jordan's problems as a baseball player were likewise fictionalized in the film.

Jordan was not credited as an actor for the first time in the film. Jordan appeared in an episode of Almost Live, a sketch comedy show located in Seattle, Washington, on November 17, 1990, according to the Internet Movie Database. He has also featured as a guest on various talk show presenters, including Oprah Winfrey, Jay Leno, and Rosie O'Donnell, and has hosted an edition of Saturday Night Live in 1991.

If you grew up in that decade, the Quad City DJs' song of the same name is almost certainly lodged in your head. Jordan was also mentioned in Michael Jackson's song Jam, in which the music video depicts Jackson teaching Jordan how to dance while Jordan teaches Jackson how to play basketball.

While today's NBA stars, such as LeBron James, are making similar strides, the jury is still out on who is better between "The King" and "His Airness." James wore number 6 for four years with the Miami Heat, sharing the historic number 23 with the Cleveland Cavaliers. James has averaged 27.3 points, 7.1 rebounds, and 6.9 assists per game during 12 professional seasons since entering the NBA at the age of 19 in 2003. Because he, like Bryant, entered the NBA straight out of high school, there's a chance he'll have a longer career than Jordan.

James has already been named to the NBA All-Star team 11 times and has won four NBA MVP honors, yet he only has two NBA Championships. There's a case to be made that someone like Kobe Bryant, who has averaged 25.4 points, 5.3 rebounds, and 5.6 assists per game across his 18 years in the NBA, should be compared to Jordan. Bryant has also won five NBA championships (2000-2002, 2009-2010). Players from the past, such as Wilt Chamberlin or Larry Bird, might potentially be involved.

Regardless of their all-time rankings, few athletes have ever had their own shoe line, several three-peat performances, or a blockbuster film like Jordan. Even Jordan has enjoyed the banter, but at 52, there's little chance we'll see him go off against Bryant or James in a one-on-one pick-up game. While it is exceedingly unlikely to occur in real life, it cannot be denied that video games and other forms of virtual reality have been utilized to simulate the possibility. Jordan is a secret character in most NBA games that can be unlocked and used in a variety of fantasy matchups that today's basketball fans fantasize about.

We may never see another athlete with such a long list of accomplishments as Jordan, a list that could continue to increase in the future, especially if the Jordan-owned Charlotte Hornets can win their first title.

# If you like what you read, Please leave a review!

I write because I enjoy sharing the inspiring stories of people like Michael Jordan with wonderful readers like you. My readers motivate me to create more, so please don't hesitate to leave a review to let me know what you thought!

# References

1. M, Daniel. "Michael Jordan: The 10 Greatest Games of His Airness." 17 Feb. 2012. Web. <http://bleacherreport.com/articles/1069931 michael-jordan-the-10-greatest-games-of-his-airness>.
2. Nathan, Alec. "23 Things Michael Jordan Gave to NBA Fans." 1 Aug.
2013.
Web.<http://bleacherreport.com/articles/1719350-23-thingsmichael-
jordan-gave-to-nba-fans/page/2>.
3. Lake, Thomas. "Did This Man Really Cut Michael Jordan?" 16 Jan.
2012.
Web.
<http://www.si.com/vault/2012/01/16/106149626/did-thisman-
really-cut-michael-jordan>.
4. Braswell, Sean. "An Air of Greatness: Michael Jordan's Freshman
Year." 3 Nov. 2014. Web. <http://www.ozy.com/flashback/an-air-ofgreatness-michael-jordans-freshman-year/34289 >.
5. Greenberg, Jon. "Portrait of a Legend." 12 Sept. 2009. Web. <http://sports.espn.go.com/chicago/columns/story?columnist=greenberg_jon&id=4468210>.
6. "NBA and ABA Leaders and Records." Web. <http://www.basketballreference.
com/leaders/>.
7. "Michael Jordan NBA Stats: Basketball Reference." Web.
<http://www.basketball-
reference.com/players/j/jordami01.html>.

Printed in Great Britain
by Amazon